Giovanni Battista Piranesi

DRAWINGS IN THE
PIERPONT MORGAN LIBRARY

DETAIL OF NO. A-1.

Giovanni Battista Piranesi

DRAWINGS IN THE PIERPONT MORGAN LIBRARY

Felice Stampfle

With a Foreword by Charles Ryskamp

DOVER PUBLICATIONS, INC., NEW YORK
in Association with
THE PIERPONT MORGAN LIBRARY

Published in Canada by General Publishing Company, Ltd., 30 Lesmill Road, Don Mills, Toronto, Ontario.
Published in the United Kingdom by Constable and Company, Ltd., 10 Orange Street, London WC2H 7EG.

Giovanni Battista Piranesi: Drawings in The Pierpont Morgan Library is a new work, first published by Dover Publications, Inc., in 1978 in association with The Pierpont Morgan Library. The chronology, principal essay and Part One of the List of Drawings are essentially revised versions of the corresponding sections of *The Pierpont Morgan Library, Drawings by Giovanni Battista Piranesi, Illustrated Catalogue of an Exhibition January 10, 1949, to March 19, 1949,* New York, 1949.

Book design by Carol Belanger Grafton

International Standard Book Number: 0-486-23714-1
Library of Congress Catalog Card Number: 78-54866

Manufactured in the United States of America
Dover Publications, Inc.
180 Varick Street
New York, N.Y. 10014

FOREWORD

It seems particularly fitting to publish this volume in 1978, the two-hundredth anniversary of the death of Giovanni Battista Piranesi. Many of the drawings presented here are illustrated for the first time and together they constitute the entire collection of drawings by Piranesi in The Pierpont Morgan Library. The Morgan collection is not only more than twice as large as any other collection of Piranesi's drawings now known, it also shows a nearly comprehensive range of his subject matter: archaeological, architectural, decorative, and visionary—drawings for books and buildings, etchings and furniture. There are designs for mantelpieces, tables, chairs, candelabra, sconces, a clock, sedan chairs and coaches, and a gondola. There are a number of his comparatively rare figure studies. The drawings range in time from his early associations with the French academicians in Rome and his return to Venice (1744–1745) to the years of the 1760's when he was involved in his one great architectural accomplishment, the restoration of Santa Maria Aventina and the Priory of the Order of Malta in Rome, and a project which was not realized, the alteration of the west end of San Giovanni in Laterano. Finally there are three monumental drawings of the late 1770's when Piranesi made trips to Pompeii and Herculaneum to study the ancient ruins.

Piranesi's series of etchings and books are represented here by preparatory studies associated with them: the *Prima parte di architetture* (1743), *Le antichità romane* (1756), *Carceri* (1756–1761), *Della magnificenza ed architettura de' Romani* (1761), *Lapides Capitolini sive fasti consulares triumphalesque Romanorum* (1762), *Antichità di Cora* and *Antichità d'Albano* (1764), *Diverse maniere d'adornare i cammini ed ogni altra parte degli edifizj* (1769), *Vasi, candelabri, cippi, sarcofagi, tripodi, lucerne,* *et ornamenti antichi* (1778), and even, perhaps, the *Seconda parte de' tempj antichi*, etched by his son Francesco (1790). The drawings illustrated that are now owned by the Morgan Library (a number of versos are shown as well as all of the rectos) are supplemented by two drawings promised to the Library from the collection of Mr. and Mrs. E. V. Thaw. The drawings are in various media: pen, black and red chalk, pencil, and wash. They range in size from mere scraps and fleeting notations to precise and elaborately realized designs; the largest is nearly five feet long. Together they brilliantly realize the essential genius of the artist.

We are thankful to Mr. and Mrs. Thaw for permitting us to include their drawings at this time when we are publishing our complete collection of drawings by Piranesi. A special debt of gratitude is owed to Miss Felice Stampfle, Curator of Drawings and Prints in The Pierpont Morgan Library, and to her associates in that Department, Mrs. Cara Dufour Denison, Mrs. Helen Mules, and Miss Mary Laura Gibbs, who helped her in preparing this volume. Most of the photographic work for this volume was accomplished at the Library by the head of the photographic department, Charles V. Passela.

Miss Stampfle first published all but twelve of these drawings just thirty years ago. Only about a third of the drawings, however, were illustrated at that time. We are pleased to dedicate this volume to the memory of Mrs. J. P. Morgan, who collected what is still by far the largest and finest collection of Piranesi drawings. Her group of 123 drawings by Piranesi and ten more which may be the work of pupils or assistants comprises all but a dozen of the drawings illustrated here.

CHARLES RYSKAMP
Director

CHRONOLOGY OF G.B. PIRANESI

1720   Born October 4 at Mogliano near Venice, the son of Angelo Piranesi, a stonemason, and Laura Lucchesi, his wife. Educated as an architect under his uncle, the architect and engineer Matteo Lucchesi, and later under the architect Scalfarotto; studied perspective with Carlo Zucchi. Possibly worked in the studios of the Bibiena and the Valeriani.

1740   Left Venice for Rome as a draughtsman in the suite of Marco Foscarini, the Venetian Ambassador to the Papal Court. Studied etching under Giuseppe Vasi.

1743   Completed his first etched series, *Prima parte di architetture e prospettive.*

1744   Forced to return to Venice because of lack of funds. Probably worked in the studio of Giovanni Battista Tiepolo at this time.

1745   Returned to Rome with the assistance of the publisher Giuseppe Wagner and eventually established himself as an etcher and publisher of Roman architecture and antiquities, producing over a thousand plates in thirty-five years. Active in artistic and archaeological circles, numbering among his friends the English architect Robert Adam, the French architect C. L. Clérisseau, and the French artist Hubert Robert.

1752   Married Angelica Pasquini by whom he had three children: Laura, Francesco, and Pietro, all active in carrying on their father's publications.

1757   Elected a Fellow of the Society of Antiquaries, London, on February 24.

1761   Received into the Academy of St. Luke, Rome.

1763–64 Visited Chiusi and Corneto, making studies of Etruscan antiquities.

1764–65 Restored the Church of Santa Maria Aventina and the Priory of the Order of Malta at the commission of Cardinal Giovanni Battista Rezzonico, Grand Prior of the Order and nephew of Pope Clement XIII.

1767   Received the title "Cavaliere degli Sproni d'Oro" from Clement XIII on January 16. Presented a series of drawings for the reconstruction of the choir of San Giovanni in Laterano to Cardinal Giovanni Battista Rezzonico.

1770   Visited Pompeii and Herculaneum in the first of various visits during the 1770's, collecting material later utilized by his son Francesco.

1777   Visited Paestum, preparing drawings of the Doric temples for the etched series completed after his death by Francesco.

1778   Died November 9. Buried in Santa Maria Aventina.

Giovanni Battista Piranesi
DRAWINGS IN THE PIERPONT MORGAN LIBRARY

Discussions of the drawings of Giovanni Battista Piranesi have invariably been prefaced by a statement of their rarity, a rarity that has always appeared paradoxical in view of the enormous graphic productivity of the great eighteenth-century etcher. Considering that the artist etched more than a thousand plates, many of them oversize, and that in numerous instances the plates must have entailed more than a single preparatory sketch, the number of his surviving drawings has appeared curiously out of proportion even when allowance was made for the scrapping of working drawings and the inevitable toll of the passing centuries. Consequently, there has always been speculation that eventually more of the drawings might come to light. Giesecke, Focillon, and Hind, the foremost authorities on Piranesi,[1] have all at various times prophesied the discovery of additional material in private collections. Their prophecies were spectacularly borne out in the appearance of a group of one hundred and thirty-three drawings formerly in the private collection of the late Mrs. J. P. Morgan. With the exception of possibly ten drawings, the group is unquestionably from the hand of Giovanni Battista Piranesi and so becomes the largest single collection of the drawings of the great architectural etcher which is of record.[2] Executed in many cases on the verso of impressions of the artist's own etchings, in some instances carrying notes in his autograph, in others easily identifiable as preparatory studies for his etched works and his architectural projects, the drawings constitute an authentic group of the greatest significance and interest for the study and appreciation of Piranesi both as a draughtsman and as an architect.

The collection as a whole is in excellent condition and gives evidence of having been well cared for over a long period. The variety and number of the drawings suggest that they may have been gathered as a unit directly from the artist's studio and preserved by a member of the family or by an early collector. This surmise also seems to be supported by the fact that so many of the drawings fall into definite groups, each connected with a specific project. There is, for example, a block of over forty sketches relating to one of the volumes of etched works. It has not been possible as yet to trace the provenance of the drawings prior to their entry into Mrs. Morgan's collection although it seems likely that they were acquired in England sometime during the first or second decade of this century.

The drawings vary widely in size, in medium, and in style of execution. Some are impressive compositions executed on paper of imperial measurements; some are the most fleeting of graphic notations set down on scraps of old letters, memoranda, even a laundry list. Some are finished drawings painstakingly set off by carefully ruled borders. There are numerous free *pensieri*, sketches supplemented by inscriptions, academic studies of details, elevations and ground plans, working drawings with measurements, drawings squared for enlargement, a tracing. Many are executed on the laid papers with the encircled fleur-de-lis watermark of the stocks upon which Piranesi's etchings were printed.[3] In a great many instances the drawings are placed on the verso of waste impressions of the etchings, the publication dates of which handily provide a reasonable *terminus post quem* for the execution of the drawing.

Piranesi's characteristic mixed technique which contributes so richly to the colorful brilliance of his style is in evidence in the many drawings executed in pen and ink over a preliminary red- and/or black-chalk sketch and frequently accompanied by brown or gray washes. In some drawings, the red chalk comes into further play to correct and supplement the pen work. There are examples of drawings in which the artist works directly with pen, particularly as he records the first ideas for the designs for decoration. Ordinarily, however, there are traces of an initial sketch in black chalk or pencil, although they may consist of no more than the most summary of outlines. The inks generally appear to be of the iron gall variety, and several of the drawings exhibit corroded passages where the ink has eaten through the paper as is its destructive tendency. Within the browns of the ink and washes, there is a very considerable fluctuation from those passages where the ink retains the depth of its original color to those where it assumes the yellow-browns of bister and again to those where the browns are of a cooler gray cast. From time to time, bister also appears to have been employed and occasional use is made of gray washes of India ink. Red and black chalks, in addition to serving as media for the light sketch underlying a pen drawing, are also used with effectiveness both singly and in combination. They seem to be the favored media for drawings preparing details, being used especially for studies from the antique and for studies of architectural detail.

The collection is well stocked with drawings characterized by the swift brilliance and boldness commonly associated with Piranesi's draughtsmanship but there is also ample representation of his equally characteristic though less usual manners. A choicely beautiful example of his typical handling of pen and wash is to be found in the drawing for a wall monument (no. 110) which is marked by the virile, outspoken accents of the rapid slashing pen line and the dramatic brushing of the washes. A more disciplined treatment distinguishes the architectural designs where an architect's precision and finished formality of draughtsmanship prevail. In this connection, a meticulously rendered plan and section of the Farnese Palace (nos. 48, 49), probably early work, perhaps reflect Piranesi's association with the French academicians in Rome for whom such projects were prescribed as a part of their training program. Drawings such as that of the villa and garden, and the fragmentary wash drawing on the verso (no. 1), or the court of no. 3 show the artist working in a gentler mood with a finely sharpened pen that produces a more subdued and regular linear pattern which he varies with soft gray washes. The sparkling style of such drawings as that of the gondola (no. 10), of the wall panels (nos. 11, 12, 13) and of the detail of the pulpit (no. 8) has a distinctive quality all its own and these drawings are set apart as the best of what might be termed Piranesi's Venetian rococo manner. The fantastic and decorative delicacy of the pen work in the last-mentioned drawing is an amazing contrast to the harsh boldness one finds in the sketch for a mantelpiece (no. 84), where Piranesi in some passages spreads the flexible pen to the width of almost a quarter of an inch.

Although the drawings span the range of Piranesi's activity with the exception of his very last years, which are represented by only one example, the greater part of them appear to date from the 1760's, the years when he was active in the service of Pope Clement XIII and other members of the Rezzonico family, and at the height of his prominence both in Rome and in Europe generally. Among the most interesting and beautiful drawings of the collection, however, are those which originate from the period of the forties when the influences of Bibiena and of Tiepolo are paramount in Piranesi's style. The earliest which can be definitely dated (no. 3) is a preparatory study, in pen and brown ink with gray wash, of the left corner of the etching "Prospetto d'un regio Cortile . . .," plate 12 of the *Prima parte di architetture* published in 1743. The drawing, which is in the reverse of the etching and on the same scale, is carried out with delicate precision and shows the solicitude with which, on occasion at least, the young artist prepared the designs for his etchings. It is true that among the early drawings in various collections there are a number of rapid pen sketches which can be identified in many instances as studies for the etchings,[4] but this is one of the few instances of the survival of such a carefully prepared drawing for one of the early etched works, though it, to be sure, survives only as a fragment. The design is of interest in its reflection of the youthful Piranesi's contact with the Bibiena style. Also in the spirit of the imaginative architectural inventions of the

Prima parte di architetture and the *Opere varie di architettura*, 1750, are two other drawings in pen and wash (nos. 2, 4) and a third in black chalk (no. 6). Freer and more spirited in their handling, they cannot be linked with any of the etched plates. The chalk drawing is a large (16 9/16 x 21 13/16 inches) rhythmic sketch of considerable power and breadth, and shows the artist experimenting with an idea for one of the great architectural complexes on the grand scale of the larger prints of the *Opere varie*.

The half-dozen or so Tiepolesque drawings form a unit of signal beauty and distinction. They include two large designs for title pages or frontispieces (nos. 7, 8) of the lavish nature that adorn the volumes of the etched works, displaying the customary rich paraphernalia of scrolls, tablets, crowns, palms, lanterns, fragments of ancient monuments, et cetera. One of the designs (no. 8) is almost deceptively close to Tiepolo in the facile flow of the warm golden-brown washes against the creamy surfaces of a paper that appropriately and significantly carries a Venetian watermark.[5] Of additional interest in this drawing is the use of a pale red watercolor wash on the ground plan at the left, the only occurrence of color in the collection.[6] With the sketch for the title page is combined another, apparently unrelated, drawing depicting with a line of rococo delicacy a design for a pulpit addorsed to a column. It has been painstakingly pricked for transfer. The second drawing for a title page (no. 7), which presents a vigorous pattern of bold accents created by a rapidly working pen, is the more complete of the two, but neither apparently was ever executed. One of the most unusual and beautiful drawings in the entire collection is the fantastic design for a festal gondola (no. 10), to be dated probably in the middle forties (*ca.* 1744) at the time Piranesi returned from Rome to Venice because of lack of funds and is said to have worked in the studio of Tiepolo.[7] In this instance, both the style and the subject of the drawing are emphatically Venetian, the style acknowledging Tiepolo, the subject recalling Guardi's *bissona* sketches, and the quality and beauty of the draughtsmanship ranking Piranesi with both his great contemporaries. With such a subject to stir him, Piranesi's pen creates with a lyric lightness of touch and conjures up an enchanted barge dripping with the foam of a magic sea and sparkling in the brilliance of Venetian sunlight. The same light and airy execution and the same fanciful manner are reflected in three drawings which appear to be designs for wall panels (nos. 11, 12, 13). Two of the drawings are obviously for the same project, but the third (no. 13), which is drawn in perspective, exhibits quite a different ornamentation. Contemplating the ornate escutcheons and the flanking sconces of the panels, one recalls the conjectures of various writers that Piranesi may have been employed in the decoration of the Venetian palaces during his periods of activity in his native city, of which so little is known.[8] Yet another drawing probably dating from the period of the forties is the capriccio (no. 9) which, with its fountain, its jumble of fallen columns, and its mourning satyrs, is related in subject matter to the four *Groteschi* of the *Opere varie*. The *Groteschi* are the etchings in which the influence of Tiepolo is most obvious in the graphic work of Piranesi, and, likewise, his influence is traceable in this drawing. Conceived on a scale comparable to that of the etchings (14 1/2 x 20 3/16 inches), the drawing is strikingly effective in its execution and hauntingly evocative in its romantic mood.

The subject matter of the famous *Carceri* series is suggested in only two of the drawings. Most nearly related to the style of the powerful etchings is a small brusque sketch (no. 15), in red chalk splashed with a brown wash, which depicts shadowy figures mounting a stairway in a great hall. It seems likely that this drawing dates from the later forties when Piranesi was preparing the etchings. The other (no. 16), which is perhaps somewhat earlier, has little connection with the *Carceri* beyond the fact that it depicts a prison. A less hastily executed drawing, it portrays in contrasting browns and grays an interior of monumental vastness laced with massive piers and heavy vaults pierced by grated oculi. The tiny figures clustering protectively in groups of twos and threes within the vast spaces are brushed in with an authority and suggestiveness akin to Rembrandt.

Perhaps also to be grouped with the early period are the two pages of delightful calligraphic pen sketches (nos. 17, 18) crisply depicting a bizarre array of temples, plazas, fanciful monuments, and various fantastic vases, all copies from Johann Bernhard Fischer von Erlach's *Entwurff einer historischen Architectur . . . ,* Vienna, 1721, as was first pointed out by Willard O. Clifford. As Piranesi turned through the plates of the famous Austrian architect's pictorial history of architecture, he systematically sketched and annotated. The fragment of a temple plan carries the note *statua/di giove.* Beside a hastily sketched column he reminds himself, *dorico/senza/involtar.* Below an idea for a marine arena he scribbles at some length, *naumachia/ornata con principali/palazzi alle parti/e nel mezo e sopra frontispici li soliti ornamen/ti di trofei statue, e cavali, cochi tirati da cavali.* He provides the stenographic indication of a car drawn by two elephants with the memorandum, *cochio/con l'imperator dentro/e fama sopra che l'/incorona—a sei elefanti.* On the verso he makes the interesting note, *colona traiana/serve per campanile,* and apropos of bulbous ornamental forms on a wall, he descriptively comments, *Bale a fette di/melon.*

Although Piranesi's custom of repeatedly coupling the title "Architetto Veneziano" with his name on the title pages of his etched works is indicative of his pride in the profession for which he was trained, his work as a practicing architect was limited. Beyond the restoration of Santa Maria Aventina, also known as Santa Maria del Priorato, and the Priory of the Order of Malta, and possibly the designing of a palace in the Via de' Prefetti in Rome,[9] the only other traces of his architectural activity are literary references. It is, therefore, of considerable interest that eleven of the drawings in the present collection are designs and sketches relating to Piranesi's few architectural undertakings. Five of the drawings in Mrs. Morgan's collection and a sixth acquired by the Library in 1952 are connected with the restoration of Santa Maria Aventina and the

Maltese Priory, the project undertaken in 1764–1765 at the commission of Cardinal Giovanni Battista Rezzonico, Grand Prior of the Order of Malta, who was Piranesi's friend, patron, and fellow Venetian. They are all designs for elements of the decoration[10] and, with one exception, are more or less similarly presented in pen and ink over preliminary outlines of black chalk, and in two instances completed with a soft gray wash. The most finished of the drawings relate to the interior decoration of the church. They are the designs for the vault (no. 50) and for the high altar (no. 51); the 1952 drawing is a small preliminary pen sketch for the altar. The design for the elaborate vault decoration, which is conceived as one continuous panel running the length of the church, prominently displays the emblems of the Order of Malta framed by a border of laurel. It is a careful and complete rendering of the lavish decorative scheme even to the indication of the system of adjoining panels, and its highly finished nature suggests that it may have been one of a series of drawings outlining the program for decoration in its entirety and intended for submission to the patron Cardinal for his approval. It is not identical in every respect with the actual decoration as finally carried out by Tommaso Righi, the sculptor who translated Piranesi's ideas into stucco. The most obvious differences are noted in such details as the disposition of the small angels, the pose of the figure of St. John, and the style of the coat-of-mail.

The large study for the lower part of the high altar is likewise a carefully prepared drawing set within a ruled border. At the bottom, a scale has been marked off, and scattered over the face of the drawing are various computations. There are also indications that after the drawing was more or less completed by the application of the gray wash, the artist worked over it again with black chalk in an effort to heighten the three-dimensional effect. Consequently, the drawing lacks the finished appearance of the previous design. It is interesting that Piranesi apparently conceived of the high altar, at least for practical working purposes of its execution in stucco and gypsum, as made up of two distinct parts: the imposing lower structure with an antique-sarcophagus form as a base (the subject of the drawing) and the plastic cloud of baroque figures which overlies the sphere rising from a second sarcophagus above the mensa. One surmises that such a drawing as this, designed to convey the general configuration and proportions of the lower part of the altar, would be supplemented by detailed studies of the ornament, which the fluttering ink strokes of the drawing never actually define but only suggest as a swag of laurel, a rinceau, or a rosette.

Two of the three drawings connected with the exterior decoration are designs for the ornamental stele which Piranesi placed along the wall of the Piazzale. Both of them carry measurements and are quite clearly working drawings. In the case of the design for the panel set between two obelisks to the right of the central stele (no. 53), only one-half of the symmetrical black-chalk design has been inked into sharp focus after the manner of a typical working drawing for which transfer or duplication of some sort is contemplated. The design itself, with its medley of musical trophies combined with the Maltese cross and components of the Rezzonico arms, i.e. the tower, the double-headed eagle, and the crescent moon, is identical with the panel as it was executed. The second drawing (no. 54) is a design for the base of the central stele and it, too, coincides exactly with the finished decoration. The third drawing (no. 52) is a free sketch for the ornament, again displaying elements of the Rezzonico arms, which is set into the outer pilasters of the façade of Santa Maria Aventina. The companion sketch for the decoration of the inner pilasters is in the British Museum.

It has always been known that Piranesi, at the commission of Pope Clement XIII, drew up designs for the alteration of San Giovanni in Laterano. This information Piranesi himself made of record in the dedication of his work *Diverse maniere d'adornare i cammini ed ogni altra parte degli edifizj*, 1769, addressed to Cardinal Giovanni Battista Rezzonico, who was a nephew of the Pope. Five of the drawings in The Pierpont Morgan Library are concerned with this project for San Giovanni in Laterano. At the time of acquisition there was no way of knowing whether or not they were among the designs which were finally submitted to Clement XIII and, as we read in the dedication, were accorded a "favorable reception" by the young Cardinal Rezzonico, although they clearly give some idea of the scope and nature of Piranesi's plans for the rebuilding of the west end of the church. The drawings submitted to the Cardinal are, we now know, the presentation series acquired in 1971 by the Avery Architectural Library, Columbia University, as the gift of Dr. and Mrs. Arthur M. Sackler. As Clement XIII died in February 1769, the year in which Piranesi published the above statement, the designs were never acted upon.[11]

The largest of the drawings (no. 55), which unfolds to a length of almost five feet, is a longitudinal section through the full length of the nave looking toward the south wall. Two-thirds of this drawing is given over to a sober transcription of the wall scheme of Borromini, who restored the church in the middle of the seventeenth century, but the proposed changes and innovations at the west end of the church are indicated in a free, dashing manner with a liberal use of washes. The difference in the handling of the two sections of the drawing is marked enough to suggest that Piranesi may have turned over to an assistant the task of reproducing Borromini's nave, he himself taking over at the point of the transept, which is shown as it exists today with the fresco of the *Ascension* by Cavaliere d'Arpino. A second drawing (no. 56), which is more finished, begins with the transept and continues through an ambulatory, which is not included in the scheme of the previous drawing. No. 55, possibly the first of the series, presents the more daring scheme. Here Piranesi boldly projected raising the roof and beginning the half-dome at the point where it leaves off in the second drawing, and here he also showed, in section, a great baldachino rising almost to the height of the nave ceiling. The second drawing would seem to indicate that such a scheme, despite its appeal to the artist's taste for effects of spatial grandeur, might present practical difficulties,[12] and

he develops a less ambitious design, maintaining the transept, choir, and apse at more or less uniform heights. Both drawings suggest a decorative system of alternating stars and medallions for the ornamentation of the half-dome. The somewhat Borrominesque flavor of the decoration was no doubt intentional on the part of Piranesi who was probably mindful of the problem of keeping the proposed new construction in harmony with the baroque nave.[13] Less detailed in character, two other drawings connected with San Giovanni in Laterano (nos. 57, 58) are effective in the combination of the deep browns of the bold pen work and a contrasting gray wash. They offer somewhat different solutions for the system of the choir wall. The smaller of the two (no. 58) is also interesting in the inclusion of a sketch, in the opposite direction, of a *putto* and several winged *putto* heads, a rare subject for Piranesi. Nos. 58 and 110, as Manfred F. Fischer recently recognized, were once part of the same sheet and the plans on the verso of each relate to the Lateran project.

The architectural projects connected with the restoration of Santa Maria Aventina and the proposed alteration of San Giovanni in Laterano witness the favor Piranesi enjoyed with the Rezzonico family, of whom it is known that in addition to Pope Clement XIII and Cardinal Giovanni Battista Rezzonico, he also served the Senator Abondio, brother of the Cardinal. His name is further linked by the biographer Legrand with the powerful Albani family, but there has been no evidence to substantiate the French writer's statement.[14] Two of the drawings in the present collection would appear to offer some proof of a connection with the Albani family. They are armorial designs (nos. 126, 127), apparently for bookplates, both of which display the fess between the molet of eight points in chief and the triple mount in base of the Albani arms, surmounted by a cardinal's hat. There are several cardinals of the Albani family contemporary with the artist but none could more fittingly commission a bookplate than Alessandro Albani, founder of the famous Albani Library. It was advisedly stated above that these drawings "would appear" to offer some proof of a connection with the Albani family because it must be noted that the style does not speak unhesitatingly for Piranesi's execution. The nervous quality of the short, interrupted stroke lacks the fluency of his line, and the washes lack his customary freedom of application. On the other hand, the assured black-chalk and wash drawing on the verso of no. 127, which likewise shows an armorial design, is more easily reconcilable. Regardless of authorship, the presence of the drawings with the Albani arms in a collection of the size of the present one may possibly be of some significance for Piranesi's connection with that family.

Some forty of the drawings are sketches and designs relating to Piranesi's large decorative publication *Diverse maniere d'adornare i cammini* which appeared in 1769 with a text in Italian, French, and English. Included are designs for mantelpieces, sedan chairs and coaches, tables, chairs, candelabra, sconces, and a clock. They amply demonstrate the great fertility of the artist's decorative invention and illustrate the considerable process of selection that preceded the choice of the designs finally to be etched. Only ten of the group are specifically preparatory for plates in the *Diverse maniere d'adornare i cammini*. Of these ten, six are studies for mantelpieces, three for sedan chairs and coaches, and one for a clock. These drawings are for the most part rapid sketches recording the germination of the design. Usually they are worked out in pen over a slight sketch in red or black chalk, but there are examples where the artist works directly with the pen. Occasionally, rudimentary forms which the artist has not taken the time to develop are interpolated by scribbled notations such as those on no. 81, where one reads opposite a caryatid form: *baco* [*Bacco*] *che tien/canestra cogliendo l'uva*, or on no. 67, where the summary suggestion of a border of portrait medallions is accompanied by the description, *medaglie/con Roma de/Cesari, trium/viri, e ditatori*. There is evidence in at least one of the drawings for mantelpieces (no. 63) that the rapid sketches in pen were probably only the first of several steps in the evolution of the final designs upon which the etchings were based. In this drawing, the main element of the decoration on either jamb of the mantelpiece, the lion paw terminating in a head, has been very carefully rendered in red chalk as if directly preparatory for translation into the graphic medium, and one can assume that it was preceded by other sketches, particularly since there is evidence of counterproofing. The ornament on the lintel, however, has not been so precisely indicated and the artist has worked over it again, this time in pen. Comparison with the etched design shows that still further changes were made before the final version and most probably this entailed the execution of yet another drawing. In passing, it might be mentioned that several of the sketches for the etched mantelpiece designs are executed on the verso of impressions of other plates from the *Diverse maniere d'adornare i cammini*, indicating the various levels at which the artist was working at one period.

In the captions below the designs in the *Diverse maniere d'adornare i cammini*, Piranesi notes that two of the mantelpieces and several of the ornamental objects were carried out as practical commissions, and it may well be that some of the drawings in the present collection were preparatory for actual execution. At least the fact that certain of the drawings carry notations such as *marmo bianco, porfido*, and *alabastro* shows that the artist was thinking of his designs in terms of real materials and the finished effect. Similarly, two sheets of what appear to be sketches for the lower body of several coaches carry numerous notes as to color, suggesting that Piranesi may have also designed and supervised the execution of such equipages for his patrons as well as etching the designs incorporated in the *Diverse maniere d'adornare i cammini*.

Piranesi's role as a decorator is further emphasized by three large designs (approximately 19 x 15 inches) for mirror frames (nos. 107–109). These again are drawings of a kind and character different from any previously known work of the artist, but the crisp quality of the pen line and the sure handling of the washes speak authoritatively and unmistakably for his execution. Two of the

drawings are light and rococo in spirit but apparently of a later period than the rococo designs for wall panels mentioned earlier as likely products of the Venetian period. The third is heavier in design. All three are finished drawings with similarly ruled borders that suggest a formal purpose, and it may well have been that the drawings were part of a decorative program prepared for a patron's inspection.

An entirely different aspect of Piranesi's activity is represented in a small group of red- and black-chalk drawings of archaeological import. Some, like the sketches of ram heads and Victories (no. 34), are probably after antique models. Others, like the design for a trophy-laden lunette (no. 35), appear to be Piranesi's adaptations of classical motifs. The drawing depicting a figure of Victory with trophies between two candelabra (no. 33) is also of the latter category. This is the only squared drawing in the collection.

Three drawings of this group are strict studies of classical architectural detail. One is a black-chalk rendering of a Corinthian capital (no. 27) and the other two, in red chalk, represent a decisively modeled egg-and-dart molding (no. 25) and an acanthus leaf (no. 26). It may be recalled in connection with the measured academic quality of these studies, so different from the artist's usual precipitate style, that it is reported by Legrand that Piranesi employed young artists for the rendering of tedious details which demanded more patience than ability.[15] These drawings of details are conceivably of the character that might have been left to assistants for execution, and it is also true that the Corinthian capital bears a resemblance to those of the Pantheon etched by Piranesi's son Francesco in the *Seconda parte de' tempj antichi*, 1790. On the other hand, the drawings are not suspect from the point of view of quality and are not inconsistent with the disciplined draughtsmanship Piranesi displays in the etched plates of an exclusively architectural and constructional nature. If any distinction is to be made, it can perhaps be said that the black-chalk drawing of the capital is slightly less incisive than the red-chalk studies.

Several sheets of studies (nos. 43–45) are devoted to sketches of the classical masks which are liberally sprinkled through the etched works as decorative adjuncts, particularly of the designs for mantelpieces. They are boldly executed directly in pen, and one senses their appeal to the dramatic nature of the artist, who portrays the grimacing countenances with obvious relish.

In addition to the drawings of mantelpieces and sedan chairs which are preparatory for the etchings, there is another somewhat miscellaneous group of drawings which are preparatory for etchings and which, like the drawings just discussed, are of an archaeological nature. They are all more or less of a fragmentary character, either because they are studies only for small specific details or because the paper on which they occur has been cut down when the verso was used to accommodate another drawing, it being Piranesi's economical custom to utilize not only the backs of waste impressions of the etchings but the reverse of discarded drawings as well. What appear to have been full-scale drawings for the etchings of the Temple of Castor, plate II of the *Antichità di Cora* (1764), and of the title page of the *Antichità d'Albano* (1764) unfortunately survive only as mutilated inconsequential fragments (nos. 66, 71), the backs of which Piranesi employed for sketching ideas for the *Diverse maniere d'adornare i cammini*. Significantly, all these drawings are executed in red chalk (occasionally supplemented by black chalk), and they appear to be numerous enough (eight) to warrant the supposition that red chalk was favored for the studies immediately preceding the etchings. Four of the drawings prepare details of the plates in *Della magnificenza ed architettura de' Romani*, 1761. Two studies for the capital with confronted sphinxes (nos. 19, 20), "In Villa Burghesiana," plate XIII, are on the exact scale of the etching and correspond fairly closely. Each shows one-half of the capital. One exhibits a certain monotony of line that would seem to mark it as a tracing or a transfer drawing of some sort, the design being repeated on either side of the thin brown paper, that has the appearance of having been oiled. The studies for the dolphin capital (no. 21), "In cavo aedium Farnesianarum," plate XVIII, and the bracket (no. 22), "Praeter Basilicam S. Petri in Vaticano," plate XIX, only approximate the size of the etchings and lack the exactness of scale of the design for the sphinx capital. They are also somewhat less precisely executed and have the aspect of drawings executed in the presence of the object. The same may be said of no. 24, a study for the base of the antique altar in the etching dedicated to Thomas Barrett in the work, *Vasi, candelabri, cippi, sarcofagi, tripodi, lucerne, ed ornamenti antichi*, 1778. It is of interest that the etching carries an inscription that the altar was in the collection of Piranesi and that its base was designed after an antique monument in the façade of the Barberini Palace. Here again between the drawing and the etching one notes a sharpening and pointing up of detail. As a study preparatory for the *Vasi, candelabri . . .*, which was published the year of Piranesi's death, this drawing is the latest in the collection; it is, in fact, the only drawing which can be definitely assigned to the period of the seventies.

The Morgan collection adds several examples to the known group of figure drawings by Piranesi. The most unusual is a black-chalk sketch of a male nude which is executed on the verso of the title-page design of no. 7. Dynamic and vigorous in concept, it shows a tall, powerful figure that thrusts itself to the outermost limits of the page. It is the counterpart on a large scale of the muscular *ignudi* which indolently grace the fantastic gondola design (no. 10). More typical is the pen sketch of a seated man which occurs on a page with one of the mantelpieces (no. 62) where the figure is poised as if ready to interpret and defend Piranesi's design with the customary fervor of the intense *ciceroni* that people the etched plates. There might also be included in the category of figure drawings a study of the head and upper body of a bearded man, portrayed in slightly varying attitudes of gesticulation (no. 122), as well as the drawing of the *putti* mentioned above in connection with no. 58.

In summary, it may be said that the Morgan collection reveals Piranesi in his overlapping roles as architect, decorator, archaeologist, and etcher, supplementing to a remarkable extent the known body of his work in its preservation of heretofore unknown or scantily represented categories of his drawings. It most notably enriches the picture of his early activity with the group of superb examples reflecting his Venetian heritage. Had these drawings alone come to light, the discovery would have been one of some moment. The impact of the great Venetian tradition has always been noted here and there in the drawings of the man who became the most important Roman artist of his century, but nowhere does it find such direct and charming expression as in these examples. The emergence in this collection of a sizable group of sketches and working drawings which are connected with Piranesi's architectural commissions is of especial interest since drawings of this order have been unknown with the exception of the British Museum fragmentary sketch of a bit of decoration for Santa Maria Aventina. While these drawings definitely implement our knowledge of Piranesi's architectural activity, at the same time they confirm the fact that he who signed himself "Architetto Veneziano" was always first and foremost the artist-etcher. It is apparent that the series of designs for San Giovanni in Laterano, beautiful and brilliant as graphic expressions, were not conceived with the concrete vision of the architect, and the working drawings for Santa Maria Aventina stress the decorative trend of his activity. The largest single group of drawings in the collection is that of the designs for decoration, and, in this instance again, it is a case of the conservation of an extensive assortment of material until now known in only a few examples. By reason of their very numbers, their varying stages of sketchiness, and their marginal jottings, the many drawings relating to the etched plates illustrating *Divers Manners of Ornamenting Chimneys and All Other Parts of Houses* are of value as a most personal record of the evolution of the artist's ideas. More unusual, however, are the separate designs for wall panels and for mirror frames which are types of Piranesi drawings utterly unfamiliar to collectors. As sketches and studies of an archaeological nature tend to be somewhat rare, it is noteworthy that the Morgan collection preserves a number of them. Principally, as has been mentioned, they reproduce single objects or details, as, for instance, masks, lamps, a column, separate figures from a relief, a capital, a molding. Of a rather academic character on the whole, these studies are perhaps less interesting artistically than some of the others. It might be added as a final word that in the inscription in Piranesi's autograph on the back of one of the drawings, the collection offers an instance of specific documentation for his authorship of the text accompanying his volumes of etched plates, a fact which has sometimes been questioned by his biographers although it is now conclusively established.[16] This inscription, which deals with Etruscan vases, appears on the verso of mantelpiece design no. 84, and is undoubtedly a page of the artist's notes for the "apologetical essay" of the *Diverse maniere d'adornare i cammini*.

With the knowledge of the existence of the Morgan collection, the illusion of rarity that has long attended the drawings of Giovanni Battista Piranesi is in part dispelled, but his position as one of the brilliant Italian draughtsmen of the eighteenth century gains rather than loses thereby. One is encouraged to speculate on the possibility of still further discoveries, perhaps the reappearance of the group of early drawings of beggars and still-life compositions reported by Bianconi, a contemporary biographer, to have been in the collection of Senator Abondio Rezzonico.[17]

During the thirty years that have elapsed since the extensive group of Piranesi drawings from the collection of Mrs. J. P. Morgan (1868–1925) was first published in the *Art Bulletin* (XXX, 1948, pp. 122–41) and then exhibited a year later at the Morgan Library, there has been much progress in Piranesi studies and a not inconsiderable number of previously unknown drawings have come to light. In more than one instance, these "new" drawings complement the holdings of the Morgan Library.

Hyatt Mayor's lively study of Piranesi in all his aspects —etcher and draughtsman, archaeologist and theorist, architect and decorator—appeared in 1952 and was followed two years later by Hylton A. Thomas' pioneering monograph on the drawings. One of the volumes in the admirable Faber & Faber drawings series produced under the editorship of Sir Karl T. Parker, it remains the only book covering the full range of Piranesi's activity as a draughtsman and provides the skeletal structure for the *catalogue raisonné* that the English architectural historian Mr. John Wilton-Ely is compiling. Mr. Mayor and the late Professor Thomas called attention to further drawings in various periodicals: the former in the Baltimore Museum *News* of October 1956, where the artist's extraordinary sketch for his own tomb was published; the latter in *Kunstmuseets Årsskrift* (1952–55, pp. 13–28), where Piranesi's drawings of Pompeii were first assembled in conjunction with the example in Copenhagen, and in the *Bulletin* of the Boymans-Van Beuningen Museum, Rotterdam (VIII, no. 1, 1957, pp. 10–20), where the museum's five drawings were discussed in detail.

Perhaps the most notable advance in Piranesi studies has been in the area of his architectural activity, with the reemergence of the great series of presentation drawings formally setting forth his proposals for the reconstruction of the choir of the church of San Giovanni in Laterano, Rome, a project never acted upon and previously represented only by the drawings in the Morgan Library (nos. 55–58, 110). The monumental presentation sequence first came to the notice of European and American scholars in the 1960's when it was in the collection of a French architect, and in 1971 it was acquired by the Avery Architectural Library of Columbia University as the handsome gift of Dr. and Mrs. Arthur M. Sackler. The series was published in 1972 by Professor Dorothea Nyberg and students on the occasion of the first exhibition of the drawings at Columbia University and again in 1975 in a revised edition entitled *The Arthur M. Sackler Collection, Piranesi Drawings and Etchings at the Avery Architectural Library, Columbia University, New York.* In 1968 the German scholar Manfred F. Fischer had already published an analysis of Piranesi's various plans for the reconstruction of the choir of San Giovanni in Laterano on the basis of the Morgan drawings. Fischer recognized that the fragments of the plans on the versos of Morgan drawings nos. 58 and 110 belonged together and were once part of the same sheet; by so doing he also rescued the fine drawing on the recto of no. 110 from the limbo of the miscellaneous group to which it had been assigned in 1948–49 for it must also be a part of the Lateran studies.

Several additional drawings connected with Piranesi's only actual architectural commission, the remodeling of Santa Maria del Priorato, the church of the Knights of Malta on the Aventine Hill, have also appeared. Two are studies for the high altar, which is represented in Mrs. Morgan's collection by the finished design for the lower section (no. 51). The small germinal sketch, now also in the Morgan Library (no. A-5) was initially published by Hyatt Mayor in his 1952 book; the larger sketch in the Kunstbibliothek, Berlin, was the subject of Heinrich Brauer's "Giovanni Battista Piranesi verwirklicht einen Traum" in *Miscellanea Bibliothecae Hertzianae*, Munich, 1961, pp. 474–77, where he also identifies a drawing for the Priorato gatehouse. The Avery Library's important manuscript account book covering Piranesi's restoration of the area of the Priorato was studied for the first time in the essay "Piranesi as an Architect" by Professor Wittkower in the catalogue of the major Piranesi exhibition at Smith College in 1961, and will in time no doubt be further analyzed *in extenso* by some future architectural historian. It might be added that another comprehensive Piranesi exhibition was held in 1961 at Turin; the catalogue compiled by Dr. Ferdinando Salamon included an impressive array of 57 drawings borrowed from European cabinets.

With the recent publication of the catalogue by Sabine Jacob of the architectural and decorative drawings in the Kunstbibliothek at Berlin (1975), the third largest single collection of Piranesi's drawings (43 in all) has become fully accessible. This important collection includes the group of 28 mantelpieces earlier published by Marianne Fischer in *Berliner Museen* (XVI, 1966, no. 2, pp. 17–24); many of them, like the very similar series in the Morgan collection, relate to the etchings of the *Diverse maniere d'adornare i cammini.* William Rieder in the *Burlington*

Magazine (cxv,1973, pp. 309–17) prepared a concordance of all the known decorative drawings relating to this etched work, including the group of drawings for commodes, etc., from the collection of Sven Gahlin. It is not only in Piranesi's drawings that his role as a decorator and antiquarian has become more widely known, but several additional actual mantelpieces have been discovered for a total of five as reported by Rieder in the *Burlington Magazine* (cxvii, 1975, pp. 582–91). A table made for Cardinal Rezzonico is now in the Minneapolis Institute of Art; another was acquired by the Rijksmuseum. The circumstances attending the purchase from Piranesi of the two candelabra, composed of antique fragments from the Villa Adriana, by Sir Roger Newdigate for the Radcliffe Library in Oxford and now in the Ashmolean Museum, are related by Michael McCarthy in the *Burlington Magazine* (cxiv, 1972, pp. 466–72), together with mention of other candelabra in the Vatican, the Louvre, and elsewhere. Further information on Piranesi's activity as a restorer and dealer, as Rieder notes, is gradually accumulating (see especially Seymour Howard in *Eighteenth-Century Studies*, vii, 1973, no. 1, pp. 40ff.).

Among other drawings that have surfaced in the last several decades are the architectural fantasies in the Library of the University of Warsaw, published by Stanislawa Sawicka in *Arte Veneta* (xvii, 1962, pp. 190–94); further examples of the exceptional figural compositions (like those in Hamburg) in the Morgan Library (no. A-3) and in a private collection in Paris along with several characteristic figure studies (Bacou, respectively pp. 36 and 14–15); the three large sheets of architectural motifs at Bayonne (Jacob Bean, *Bayonne, Musée Bonnat: Les dessins italiens de la collection Bonnat*, Paris, 1960, nos. 111–13); the large capriccio of buildings in a classical seaport acquired by a private collector in New England (sold Christie's, London, 30 March 1971, no. 145); and the drawing for the *Prima parte di architetture*, 1743, published by Erichsen in *Pantheon* (xxxiv, 1976, no. 3, pp. 212–16) and subsequently acquired by an American collector. Andrew Robison in studies published in *Master Drawings* (xi, 1973, no. 4, pp. 389–92, and xv, 1977, no. 4,

pp. 387–400) has pointed out previously unnoticed connections of known drawings with the etched *oeuvre*, including three British Museum drawings related to the *Prima parte* and a detail of the Morgan Library's *Gondola* (no. 10) which Piranesi capriciously transferred to a carriage in the etching "Veduta della Basilica e Piazza di S. Pietro" (Focillon 787).

To mark the two hundredth anniversary of Piranesi's death, major exhibitions have been organized at the Hayward Gallery, London, the National Gallery, Washington, D.C., and the Fondazione Giorgio Cini in Venice. It is in observance of this anniversary that the present work is published and the greater part of the Library's holdings placed on exhibition. The Morgan series still remains the largest single group of Piranesi's drawings that is known and in this anniversary year it seemed appropriate to make reproductions of these drawings available in much greater numbers than has ever been done before in one publication. The inclusion of selected references will enable the interested reader to note what further information has accumulated in connection with individual drawings. In addition, the ten drawings that have been added to the group originally owned by Mrs. Morgan are described and illustrated, along with two drawings promised as future gifts by Mr. and Mrs. Eugene V. Thaw. Strangely enough, no clue as to the provenance of Mrs. Morgan's drawings has been forthcoming in the past thirty years. One surmise is that they may have been acquired from B. T. Batsford, the London architectural book publishers and booksellers, with whom she sometimes dealt, since Herbert Batsford appears to have had an informed interest in Piranesi. A friend of Arthur M. Samuel, Batsford prepared Samuel's book on Piranesi for publication (London, 1910) and in so doing is said to have discovered an early unknown state of one of the *Carceri* (Hector Bolitho, ed., *A Batsford Century 1843–1943*, 1943, p. 46). Mrs. Morgan's Piranesi drawings came to the Morgan Library in 1966 through the generosity of her sons, the late Mr. Junius S. Morgan and Mr. Henry S. Morgan.

FELICE STAMPFLE

NOTES

For helpful suggestions and advice, I wish to thank Dr. Jakob Rosenberg and Miss Agnes Mongan of the Fogg Museum of Art, and Dr. Richard Krautheimer of Vassar College. I am also indebted to the late Mr. Hylton A. Thomas, especially for the privilege of examining the extensive collection of photographs he assembled for his catalogue of Piranesi drawings, which was published in 1954 (see the List of Abbreviations that precedes the List of Drawings). Without access to his photographs, it would have been impossible to make a number of statements regarding the relation of the Morgan collection to the whole of Piranesi's surviving works. Photographs of Santa Maria Aventina were secured through the kind offices of Dr. Charles R. Morey, Cultural Relations Officer of the American Embassy in Rome. For the transcription of the inscriptions on the drawings, I am indebted to Dr. George K. Boyce and Miss Meta Harrsen, and to Miss Mirella d'Ancona of New York University.

1. Albert Giesecke, *Giovanni Battista Piranesi* (Meister der Graphik, vi), Leipzig, 1911. Henry Focillon, *Giovanni Battista*

Piranesi: Essai de catalogue raisonné de son oeuvre, Paris, 1918, and *Giovanni Battista Piranesi, 1720–1778*, Paris, 1918 (nouvelle édition, 1928). Arthur M. Hind, *Giovanni Battista Piranesi*, London, 1922.

2. Previously, the largest single collection known appears to have been the group of fifty-two drawings in the British Museum. Mr. Thomas informed me that, exclusive of the Morgan collection, he located a total of about three hundred and fifty drawings attributed to Piranesi, of which possibly fifty to sixty are not acceptable.

3. Hind, *op. cit.*, p. 34.

4. *Ibid.*, p. 21.

5. C. M. Briquet, *Les filigranes*, Geneva, 1907, no. 738.

6. Piranesi's biographer Legrand (*Notice historique sur la vie et les ouvrages de G. B. Piranesi*, Manuscrits, Nouvelles Acquisitions Françaises 5968, Paris, Bibl. Nationale) in the passage quoted by Henri Focillon, *G. B. Piranesi*, Paris, 1928, p. 197, makes a reference to color: "La vérité et la vigueur de ses effets, la juste projection de ses ombres et leur transparence, ou d'heureuses licences à cet égard,

l'indication même des tons de couleur sont dues à l'observation exacte qu'il allait en faire sur nature, soit au soleil brûlant, soit au clair de la lune. . . ." It may be, however, that the reference here is to tonal values in the etchings rather than to the use of watercolor in the drawings.

7. Focillon, *op. cit.*, p. 47.

8. Giesecke, *op. cit.*, p. 14; Focillon, *op. cit.*, p. 47; Werner Körte, "Giovanni Battista Piranesi als praktischer Architekt," *Zeitschrift für Kunstgeschichte*, II, 1933, p. 17.

9. Körte, *op. cit.*, pp. 30–32.

10. It has been shown, however, that Piranesi's restoration was not limited to the decoration but also involved such practical technical tasks as the shoring up of the foundations and a certain amount of rebuilding and repairs of the walls and vaulting. *Ibid.*, pp. 17–20.

11. The west end of the church, i.e. the apse end, as San Giovanni follows the primitive basilican orientation, was eventually rebuilt in the last quarter of the nineteenth century under Leo XIII.

12. Dr. Richard Krautheimer pointed out to the writer that the difficult terrain would have made it exceedingly hard to carry out the construction of the lofty apse and choir indicated in no. 55. He also made the interesting observation that Piranesi's idea of inserting a forechoir seems to anticipate the project actually executed more than a hundred years later under Leo XIII, and that it would seem, therefore, that the complaint of the canons to the effect that they did not have enough space within the simple apse of the old plan dates back at least to the eighteenth century.

13. An instance of Piranesi's awareness of a similar problem is recorded in his memorandum addressed to Raphael Mengs as head of the Academy of St. Luke, which is cited by Focillon, *op. cit.*, p. 104. Here the artist, who was violently involved in a controversy over Tommaso Righi's design for a tomb to be erected in the Academy's Church of St. Luke, stresses the necessity of doing nothing that is not in accord with the art of Pietro da Cortona.

14. *Ibid.*, p. 61, footnote.

15. *Ibid.*, p. 199.

16. See Rudolf Wittkower, "Piranesi's *Parere su l'architettura*," *Journal of the Warburg Institute*, II, 1938–39, pp. 146–158.

17. Focillon, *op. cit.*, p. 74.

LIST OF ABBREVIATIONS

These are the short-form references to publications used in the List of Drawings that follows.

Bacou, 1974.
Roseline Bacou, *Piranèse, Gravures et dessins*, Paris, 1974.

Berlin Kunstbibliothek, 1975.
Sabine Jacob, *Italienische Zeichnungen der Kunstbibliothek, Berlin, Architektur und Dekoration 16. bis 18. Jahrhundert*, Berlin, 1975. The group of Piranesi drawings included here was earlier published by Marianne Fischer in *Berliner Museen*, XVI, no. 2, 1966, pp. 17–24.

Columbia, 1972.
Avery Architectural Library, Columbia University, New York, *Giovanni Battista Piranesi*, exhibition catalogue by Dorothy Nyberg and students, 1972. See also *The Arthur M. Sackler Collection, Piranesi Drawings and Etchings at the Avery Architectural Library, Columbia University, New York*, New York, 1975 (revised edition of 1972 catalogue).

Corfiato, 1951.
Hector O. Corfiato, *Piranesi Compositions*, London, 1951.

Drawings from New York Collections, III, 1971.
Metropolitan Museum of Art, New York, *Drawings from New York Collections*, III: *The Eighteenth Century in Italy*, exhibition catalogue by Jacob Bean and Felice Stampfle, 1971.

Erichsen, 1976.
Johannes Erichsen, "Eine Zeichnung zu Piranesis 'Prima Parte,'" *Pantheon*, XXXIV, no. 3, 1976, pp. 212–16.

Fischer, 1968.
Manfred F. Fischer, "Die Umbaupläne des Giovanni Battista Piranesi für den Chor von S. Giovanni in Laterano," *Münchner Jahrbuch der bildenden Kunst*, XIX, 1968, pp. 207–28.

Mayor, 1952.
A. Hyatt Mayor, *Giovanni Battista Piranesi*, New York, 1952.

Morgan Library, *First* [and subsequent] *Fellows Report*.
The Pierpont Morgan Library, New York, *First Report to the Fellows of the Pierpont Morgan Library*, New York, 1950, etc. (*Reports* edited by Frederick B. Adams through 1968; by Charles Ryskamp 1969 to date; entries on drawings by Felice Stampfle).

Rieder, 1973.
William Rieder, "Piranesi's *Diverse Maniere*," *Burlington Magazine*, CXV, 1973, pp. 309–17.

Rieder, 1975.
William Rieder, "Piranesi at Gorhambury," *Burlington Magazine*, CXVII, 1975, pp. 582–91.

Robison, 1973.
Andrew Robison, "Piranesi's Ship on Wheels," *Master Drawings*, XI, 1973, no. 4, pp. 389–92.

Robison, 1977.
Andrew Robison, "Preliminary Drawings for Piranesi's Early Architectural Fantasies," *Master Drawings*, XV, 1977, no. 4, pp. 387–400.

Scott, 1975.
Jonathan Scott, *Piranesi*, London-New York, 1975.

Smith, 1961.
Smith College Museum of Art, Northampton, Massachusetts, *Piranesi*, exhibition catalogue by Robert O. Parks and essays by Philip Hofer, Karl Lehmann, and Rudolf Wittkower, 1961.

Thomas, 1954.
Hylton Thomas, *The Drawings of Giovanni Battista Piranesi*, London, 1954.

Watson, 1965.
F. J. B. Watson, "A Masterpiece of Neo-Classic Furniture: a Side-Table Designed by Piranesi," *Burlington Magazine*, CVII, 1965, pp. 101–02.

Wilton-Ely, 1976.
  John Wilton-Ely, "Piranesian Symbols on the Aventine," *Apollo*, CIII, 1976, pp. 214–27.

Wilton-Ely, 1978.
  Arts Council of Great Britain at the Hayward Gallery,
  London, *Piranesi*, exhibition catalogue by John Wilton-
  Ely, 1978.

LIST OF DRAWINGS

PART ONE: The Collection of Mrs. J. P. Morgan

Bequest of Junius S. Morgan and Gift of Henry S. Morgan, 1966

The drawings have been arranged here on the basis of subject matter with the exception of the group of early drawings which appear to belong to the decade of the forties. There are, accordingly, in addition to the early works, a fair-sized group of drawings of more or less archaeological significance, a smaller group of architectural drawings, an extensive assembly of designs for decorative projects, and a miscellaneous assortment including the drawings of which the attribution to Piranesi is questioned. To a certain extent, such an arrangement of the drawings by subject has some chronological sequence: it so happens that the few datable archaeological drawings relate to the etched work of the early sixties; the architectural projects were executed in the middle and later sixties; and the designs for mantelpieces and other decorative objects belong to the period preceding 1769. Measurements unless otherwise indicated have been taken along the left and lower margins. If not specifically designated as by another hand, inscriptions may be assumed to be in Piranesi's autograph. In transcribing the inscriptions, . . . has been used to indicate illegible words; [. . .] to indicate lost words; and italics to indicate deletion in the original. The letter "F" followed by a number after the description of an etched plate refers to the number in Henri Focillon, G. B. Piranesi: *Essai de catalogue raisonné de son oeuvre*, Paris, 1918. The Briquet references in regard to watermarks are to entries in C. M. Briquet, *Les filigranes*, Geneva, 1907.

EARLY PERIOD, 1740–1750

1. VILLA AND GARDEN.
   Verso: FRAGMENT OF PRISON SKETCH.
   Pen and gray-brown ink with gray-brown wash over black chalk. 4 7/8 x 7 9/16 inches (124 x 190 mm.).

2. ARCHITECTURAL COMPLEX: Section of court with Pantheon-like structure and triumphal column at right.
   Verso: FRAGMENTS OF PLANS.
   Pen and brown ink, wash, over black chalk. 7 1/2 x 5 9/16 inches (192 x 142 mm.). Watermark: Fleur-de-lis in double circle with letter v below. Inscribed at lower right: statua/a cavalo.

3. CORNER OF COURT WITH FOUR FIGURES.
   Pen and brown ink with India-ink wash; faint traces of black chalk. 5 7/8 x 5 1/2 inches (149 x 141 mm.). Inscribed on verso: camicetta/un farsetto/due paia calce/un paio manicotti/corralini [collarini?] N°4/ fazletti N°1/sugamano.
   Study (in reverse) for left corner of etching "Pro-

spetto d'un regio Cortile nel cui mezzo vi stà una Loggia tra i cui intercolonnj si veggono Fontane, Statue, ed altri ornamenti," *Prima parte di architetture*, 1743. F. 11.
   Bibliography: Erichsen, 1976, p. 212; Robison, 1977, pp. 394, 400, note 10.

4. ARCHITECTURAL COMPLEX WITH ORNAMENTAL TROPHY AT LEFT.
   Verso: RUDE SKETCH OF COLONNADE.
   Pen and brown ink, wash, over black chalk. Verso, black chalk. 10 1/16 x 7 1/16 inches (256 x 181 mm.).
   Bibliography: Mayor, 1952, fig. 40; Thomas, 1954, no. 42; *Drawings from New York Collections*, III, 1971, no. 225, repr.

5. INTERIOR WITH ARCHES AND PIERS.
   Verso: INTERIOR WITH CIRCULAR COLONNADE AND FOUNTAIN.
   Pen and brown ink, wash; traces of black chalk. Verso, pen and brown ink, wash, with additions in red chalk. 7 3/16 x 10 inches (184 x 255 mm.). Inscribed

on verso: (above) finestre; (center) colone cadu-te/nell' aqua/con altra fontana e/travio (?) principale/le basi che mese/ne sia o mese non; (below) scalini.

6. ARCHITECTURAL COMPLEX OF GALLERIES AND ARCADES WITH NICHES, TROPHIES, OCULI, etc.

Black chalk. 16 9/16 x 21 13/16 inches (421 x 555 mm.). Watermark: Fleur-de-lis in circle with letters ᴄᴬᴄ above and letter ꜰ below.

7. DESIGN FOR TITLE PAGE: Scroll surmounted by crown and foliage; corner of sarcophagus, sistrum, lantern, portrait medallion, feather, fasces, etc.

Verso: STANDING NUDE MALE FIGURE.

Pen and brown ink, wash, over black chalk; smudges of red chalk. Verso, black chalk. 15 1/2 x 20 7/16 inches (395 x 519 mm.). Watermark: Fleur-de-lis in circle with letters ᴄᴬᴄ above and letter ꜰ below.

Bibliography: Thomas, 1954, p. 17 and no. 14; *Drawings from New York Collections*, III, 1971, no. 220, repr.; Bacou, 1974, p. 30; Robison, 1977, pp. 387, 400, note 5; Wilton-Ely, 1978, under no. 9.

8. DESIGN FOR TITLE PAGE: Scroll and tablet with dove (?) and chain of medallions; at center, design for pulpit addorsed to column with ground plan at left.

Pen and golden-brown wash over black chalk; red watercolor wash in ground plan at left. 20 x 29 3/8 inches (508 x 750 mm.). Watermark: Bow and arrow. Briquet 738.

Bibliography: Thomas, 1954, under no. 14; *Drawings from New York Collections*, III, 1971, no. 221, repr.; Scott, 1975, p. 14, fig. 7; Robison, 1977, pp. 387, 400, note 5; Wilton-Ely, 1978, no. 9.

9. CAPRICCIO: Ruins with fountain, fallen columns, satyrs, etc.

Pen and brown ink, wash, over black chalk. 14 1/2 x 20 3/16 (top margin) inches (368 x 512 mm.). Watermark: Bow and arrow. Briquet 738. Inscribed at lower left: tronco/grando [girando?]/per terra/ò sia terrano.

Bibliography: Thomas, 1954, under no. 14; *Drawings from New York Collections*, III, 1971, no. 222, repr.; Scott, 1975, p. 51, fig. 59; Robison, 1977, pp. 387, 400, note 5.

10. GONDOLA.

Verso: SKETCHY SUGGESTIONS OF ORNAMENT WITH SUN AND STAR MOTIFS. DESIGN FOR DECORATIVE FRAMES.

Pen and brown ink, wash, over black chalk. Verso: Ornament, black chalk; frames, pen and brown ink over black chalk; also red chalk. 11 5/8 x 26 13/16 inches (296 x 683 mm.). Watermark: Bow and arrow. Briquet 738.

Bibliography: Mayor, 1952, p. 6, fig. 2; Thomas, 1954, p. 17 and no. 16; *Drawings from New York Collections*, III, 1971, no. 219, repr.; Robison, 1973, pp. 389–92, pl. 47, fig. 1; Scott, 1975, p. 14, fig. 8; Wilton-Ely, 1978, no. 11, repr.

11. DESIGN FOR WALL PANEL: Rococo shield with sconces at either side.

Pen and brown ink, wash, over black chalk. 11 9/16 x 9 5/16 inches (293 x 237 mm.). Watermark: Bow and arrow. Briquet 738.

Bibliography: Thomas, 1954, under no. 15; Wilton-Ely, 1978, under no. 10.

12. DESIGN FOR WALL PANEL: Rococo shield with smaller flanking shields; winged female figure at left of large shield.

Verso: SKETCH FOR TABLE.

Pen and brown ink, wash, over black chalk. 12 13/16 x 14 3/4 inches (325 x 375 mm.). Watermark: Bow and arrow. Briquet 738.

Bibliography: Mayor, 1952, p. 5, fig. 3; Thomas, 1954, p. 19 and no. 15; *Drawings from New York Collections*, III, 1971, no. 223, repr.; Wilton-Ely, 1978, no. 10.

13. WALL PANEL: Ornamental moldings with medallion at bottom supported by seated winged figures.

Pen and brown ink, wash, over black chalk. 11 5/16 x 11 1/16 inches (288 x 282 mm.).

Bibliography: Thomas, 1954, under no. 15; *Drawings from New York Collections*, III, 1971, no. 224, repr.; Wilton-Ely, 1978, under no. 10.

14. DECORATIVE SHELL (?) FORM.

Pen and brown ink, wash, over black chalk. 9 11/16 x 7 1/4 inches (246 x 184 mm.). Watermark: Deer within a scalloped medallion.

Bibliography: Mayor, 1952, fig. 6; Thomas, 1954, no. 12.

15. PRISON INTERIOR: Figures mounting stairway.

Red chalk with gray-brown wash; few lines in pen. 8 7/16 x 5 15/16 inches (215 x 152 mm.). Watermark (fragmentary): Tip of shield with double floral chains supporting medallions and Maltese cross.

16. PRISON INTERIOR: Great hall with heavy piers and arches pierced by grated oculi; figures in foreground.

Pen and brown ink with India-ink wash over black chalk. 7 3/16 x 9 11/16 inches (183 x 246 mm.).

Bibliography: Corfiato, 1951, pl. 50; *Drawings from New York Collections*, III, 1971, no. 218, repr.; Bacou, 1974, p. 67.

17. SHEET OF SKETCHES AFTER FISCHER VON ERLACH: Temples, tombs, sarcophagi, circus, ground plans, vases, etc.

Verso: LAYOUT OF FORMAL GARDEN.

Pen and brown ink. 16 3/8 x 11 1/8 inches (418 x 283 mm.). Watermark: Fleur-de-lis in double circle. Inscribed: (above) statua/di giove—cochio con cavali.—a buo (?)—tempio; (center) tempio—trofei-dorico/senza/involtar/lita (?)—naumachia/ naumachia/ornata con principali/palazzi alle parti e nel mezo e sopra frontispici li soliti ornamen/ti di trofei statue, e cavali, cochi tirati da cavali—cochio/con l'imperator dentro/e fama sopra che l'/incorona—a sei elefanti—Apoleo—rose—vaso con due rechie/per manico; (below) trofei—arco/arco—elefanti/con cochio—arco e pure/nella fronte—soldato—animal/egizio/virile/alla veta. Verso: colona traiana/serve per campanile—per . . . taldo bale a fette di/melon.

Bibliography: Corfiato, 1951, pl. 56; Mayor, 1952, p.

3; Thomas, 1954, p. 16 and no. 3; Smith, 1961, no. 22, p. 100, pl. 47; *Drawings from New York Collections*, III, 1971, no. 216, repr.; Wilton-Ely, 1978, no. 25.

18. SHEET OF SKETCHES AFTER FISCHER VON ERLACH: Forum with equestrian statue and fountain, and plan; vases.

 Verso: VILLA AND GARDEN: Perspective view showing entrance with fountains, row of poplars, etc. Above, colonnade.

 Pen and brown ink. Verso, black chalk, and pen and brown ink. 16 5/16 x 11 1/16 inches (415 x 282 mm.). Inscribed: cochio tirato da cavali/trofei E fama che incorona— . . . —trofei—trofei—cochio—due cavali/tenuti da un/soldato/sopra—s[ta]tua del/imperatore—arco.

 Bibliography: Mayor, 1952, p. 3; Wilton-Ely, 1978, under no. 25.

ARCHAEOLOGICAL

19. CAPITAL WITH CONFRONTED SPHINXES.

 Red chalk over black. 3 1/2 x 5 7/16 inches (90 x 139 mm.).

 This drawing and No. 20 are preparatory designs for the etching of the capital labeled "In Villa Burghesiana, et penes D. Belisarium Amadei in Foro Navonio," pl. XIII of *Della magnificenza ed architettura de' Romani*, 1761. F. 945. The sphinx at the right is a red-chalk tracing.

20. CAPITAL WITH CONFRONTED SPHINXES: Right half.

 Verso: SAME SUBJECT IN REVERSE.

 Red chalk. 3 1/16 x 3 3/8 inches (78 x 91 mm.).

 The designs on both the recto and the verso are tracings. The paper gives the appearance of having been oiled.

21. DOLPHIN CAPITAL.

 Verso: ARCHITECTURAL FRAGMENT WITH SPHINX HEADS AND PUTTI.

 Red chalk with few outlines in black. Verso, red chalk over black. 4 x 9 inches (103 x 230 mm.).

 Preparatory study for etching of capital labeled "In cavo aedium Farnesianarum" at upper left of pl. XVIII, *Della magnificenza ed architettura de' Romani*, 1761. Etching is not listed by Focillon.

 Bibliography: Smith, 1961, no. 161.

22. BRACKET.

 Verso: FRAGMENTS OF ORNAMENT.

 Red chalk. 9 5/16 x 2 1/2 (upper margin) inches (237 x 64 mm.).

 Study for etching of bracket labeled "Praeter Basilicam S. Petri in Vaticano," pl. XIX, *Della magnificenza ed architettura de' Romani*, 1761. The drawing is in the same direction and on the same scale as the etching. Etching is not listed by Focillon.

 Bibliography: Smith, 1961, no. 162.

23. DECORATIVE SHIELD: Ornament of shell, signs of Zodiac, garland, and acorn border.

 Verso: PLATFORM WITH STEPS.

Red chalk over black; pen work at lower right. Verso, black chalk. 5 3/4 x 5 11/16 inches (147 x 146 mm.). Watermark: Anchor in circle with letter M below.

 Study for a detail of the etched title page of *Lapides Capitolini sive fasti consulares triumphalesque Romanorum* [1762]. F. 421. In the etching the acorn border has been discarded and the head of Medusa substituted for the shell motif used in the drawing.

 Bibliography: Smith, 1961, no. 160.

24. FRIEZE MOTIF: Standing *putti* with swag of fruit.

 Verso: FLYING PUTTI.

 Red and black chalk. Verso, red chalk. 4 3/4 x 11 3/16 inches (121 x 285 mm.).

 Study for detail of etching dedicated to Thomas Barrett and inscribed "Altare antico di marmo ritrovato fra le macerie della Villa Adriana nel sito detto Pantanello," *Vasi, candelabri, cippi, sarcofagi, tripodi, lucerne, ed ornamenti antichi*, 1778. According to the rest of the inscription, the altar was in the collection of Piranesi, and its base, which is the subject of this drawing, was designed after an antique monument in the façade of the Barberini Palace.

25. EGG-AND-DART MOLDING.

 Red chalk. 4 13/16 x 13 3/8 inches (123 x 340 mm.).

 Watermark: Fleur-de-lis in circle with mark CB below.

 Bibliography: Mayor, 1952, p. 33, rejects Piranesi's authorship of drawings of this kind.

26. ACANTHUS LEAF.

 Red chalk. 7 5/16 x 11 15/16 inches (186 x 302 mm.).

27. CORINTHIAN CAPITAL.

 Black chalk. 15 7/16 x 10 1/2 inches (393 x 267 mm.). Watermark: Fleur-de-lis in double circle.

28. FUNERARY MONUMENT: Front view with dolphins and swag framing inscription reading DM/EUTYCHIAE/NICOSTRATUS/CONIUX/BMF; detail of dolphin (opposite direction).

 Red chalk. 10 7/8 x 8 3/8 (top margin) inches (277 x 213 mm.). Watermark: Fleur-de-lis in circle with small modified fleur-de-lis above.

 Bibliography: Smith, 1961, no. 157.

29. CLASSICAL HEAD; TWO HEADS OF RAMS.

 Verso: proof impression (before inscription, here lettered in ink) of etching, pl. 4 of *Le rovine del Castello dell' Acqua Giulia*, 1761. F. 405.

 Red chalk. Preliminary black-chalk outlines in classical head. 5 3/8 x 6 13/16 inches (137 x 173 mm.).

 Bibliography: Thomas, 1954, no. 80; Smith, 1961, no. 159.

30. FOUR ANTIQUE LAMPS: Interior designs of charioteer, Eros as hunter, two animals on a vase, two dolphins.

 Red chalk. 9 3/4 x 7 inches (248 x 178 mm.).

 Lamps with dolphin and Eros motifs appear on pl. XIII of vol. II of *Le antichità romane*, 1756.

31. HEAD OF BEARDED MAN THREE-QUARTERS LEFT.
    Verso: DECORATIVE DESIGN (fragment).
    Red chalk. Verso, black chalk. 6 1/2 x 4 5/16 inches
    (166 x 110 mm.).

32. HEAD OF BEARDED MAN THREE-QUARTERS RIGHT.
    Red chalk. 6 1/2 x 4 3/8 inches (165 x 112 mm.).
    After sculpture.

33. FRIEZE: Figure of Victory with palm, trophies, and can-
    delabra.
    Red chalk; squared in black chalk. 8 1/2 x 16 1/8
    inches (216 x 410 mm.). Watermark: Fleur-de-lis in
    double circle with mark CB above.

34. STUDIES FROM THE ANTIQUE: Two rams' heads and
    nose of third; two single figures of Victory; warrior with
    Phrygian cap supporting nude youth holding double-
    headed ax; Victories with trophy.
    Red and black chalk. 18 5/16 x 13 3/4 inches (466 x
    351 mm.). Watermark: Fleur-de-lis in double circle.

35. LUNETTE WITH TROPHIES; WINGED SERPENTS AND DOL-
    PHINS IN SPANDRELS.
    Red chalk over black; corrections in helmet in black
    chalk. 10 7/16 x 22 inches (266 x 560 mm.). Water-
    mark: Fleur-de-lis in single circle with letter v below.

36. FRIEZE MOTIF: Winged head supported by seated
    putto.
    Pen and brown ink over black chalk; smudges of red
    chalk. 2 15/16 x 9 1/4 inches (75 x 235 mm.).

37. SKETCH AFTER ANTIQUE RELIEF WITH FOUR HEADS,
    TORCHES, AND STARS.
    Black chalk; base line in red chalk. 7 x 5 3/4 inches
    (179 x 145 mm.).

38. PEDIMENTED NICHE WITH FRIEZE BELOW.
    Black chalk. 8 11/16 (right margin) x 5 1/4 inches
    (206 x 134 mm.). Watermark: Fleur-de-lis in double
    circle with mark CB above.

39. LION-CLAW PEDESTAL AND SHALLOW URN: Front and
    profile views.
    Black chalk. 6 13/16 x 8 1/2 inches (174 x 217
    mm.). Watermark: Fleur-de-lis in single circle.

40. HORNED GROTESQUE WITH PROTRUDING TONGUE.
    Red chalk. 2 5/16 x 2 13/16 inches (60 x 69 mm.).
    Similar to head on capital in etching labeled "E
    regione aedis ss. Nerei et Achillei," pl. XIX, *Della ma-
    gnificenza ed architettura de' Romani*, 1761.

41. CLASSICAL WEAPONS: Scabbard, swords, ax, spear, etc.
    Black chalk. 10 3/4 x 13 5/16 inches (273 x 339
    mm.). Watermark: Fleur-de-lis in circle with small
    modified fleur-de-lis above, the letter B below.

42. SKETCH OF CAPITAL WITH DOLPHIN AND ACANTHUS.
    Verso: ANIMAL CLAW AND LEG (DETAIL OF FURNI-
    TURE). PUTTO HEAD. ROCOCO PANEL.
    Pencil. Verso, black chalk. 5 x 9 9/16 inches (127 x
    244 mm.).

43. SIX MASKS.
    Verso: HORSE AND RIDER WITH SHIELD AND SPEAR.
    PEDIMENTED NICHE.
    Pen and brown ink. Verso, black chalk. 8 x 13 7/16
    inches (203 x 342 mm.). Inscribed at upper right: B.P.
    Verso, in niche: Mezzo. Not Piranesi's hand.

44. THREE MASKS: Executed over sketch of sandaled foot.
    Verso: SANDALED FOOT.
    Pen and brown ink; sketch of foot in black chalk.
    Verso, black chalk. 7 7/8 x 10 1/8 inches (201 x 258
    mm.).

45. MASK.
    Pen and brown ink. 4 1/4 x 3 1/8 inches (107 x 79
    mm.).

46. COLUMN: Figural decoration at base and other orna-
    ment in relief.
    Pen and brown ink over black chalk. 10 5/8 x 2 11/16
    inches (271 x 68 mm.).
    Bibliography: Smith, 1961, no. 19.

47. SKETCHES OF MOLDINGS.
    Verso: PEDESTAL WITH SPHINX BASE EXECUTED OVER
    OUTLINE SKETCH OF LION.
    Black chalk and pen and brown ink. Verso, pen and
    dark brown ink over black chalk; lion sketched in black
    chalk. 7 7/8 x 11 7/8 inches (210 x 320 mm.).

ARCHITECTURAL

48. FARNESE PALACE: Longitudinal section.
    Pen and brown ink with India-ink wash. 8 3/4 x
    12 11/16 inches (222 x 323 mm.). Courtyard doorway
    cut out.
    Bibliography: Corfiato, 1951, pl. 63; Wilton-Ely,
    1978, no. 55.

49. FARNESE PALACE: Ground plan.
    Pen and brown ink with India-ink wash. 8 3/4 x
    12 13/16 inches (222 x 325 mm.).
    Bibliography: Wilton-Ely, 1978, under no. 55.

50. SANTA MARIA AVENTINA (also called SANTA MARIA DEL
    PRIORATO): Panel with emblems of the Order of Malta.
    Pen and brown ink with India-ink wash; traces of
    black chalk. 20 7/8 x 12 1/2 inches (532 x 317 mm.).
    Design for the stucco decoration of the central panel
    of the vault of Santa Maria Aventina, church of the
    Order of Malta in Rome, which, with the Priory, was
    restored by Piranesi in 1764–1765 at the commission of
    Cardinal Rezzonico. See also nos. 51–54 and A-5.
    Bibliography: Corfiato, 1951, pl. 64; Mayor, 1952, fig.
    94; Thomas, 1954, under no. 46; Smith, 1961, no. 62,
    pp. 104–05, pl. 52; *Drawings from New York Collec-
    tions*, III, 1971, no. 227, repr.; Wilton-Ely, 1976, pp.
    220–21, 225, fig. 21; Wilton-Ely, 1978, no. 234, repr.

51. SANTA MARIA AVENTINA: Design for lower part of high
    altar with antique-sarcophagi forms surmounted by
    sphere and Lamb of God.
    Pen and brown ink with India-ink wash over black

chalk; additions in black chalk and pencil (monogram). 18 9/16 x 14 3/8 inches (472 x 365 mm.). Watermark: Fleur-de-lis in single circle with letter v above. Computations at upper left and right. Scale at bottom.

The drawing showing the upper section of the altar is in the Kunstbibliothek, Berlin.

Bibliography: Mayor, 1952, fig. 92; Thomas, 1954, under no. 46; Smith, 1961, no. 59, pp. 104–05, pl. 50; *Drawings from New York Collections*, III, 1971, no. 229, repr.; Berlin Kunstbibliothek, 1975, under no. 858; Scott, 1975, p. 219, fig. 249; Wilton-Ely, 1976, pp. 220, 225, fig. 19; Wilton-Ely, 1978, no. 233, repr.

52. SANTA MARIA AVENTINA: Ornaments showing scabbard with animal head and insignia of the Rezzonico family.

Pen and brown ink over black chalk. 6 1/4 x 2 13/16 inches (159 x 72 mm.).

Sketch for panel set in outermost pilasters of the façade of Santa Maria Aventina. A similar drawing for the panel set in the inner pilasters is in the British Museum.

Bibliography: Mayor, 1952, fig. 83; Thomas, 1954, under no. 46; Wilton-Ely, 1976, pp. 220, 225, fig. 13; Wilton-Ely, 1978, under no. 310b.

53. SANTA MARIA AVENTINA: Vertical panel with Maltese cross and insignia of Rezzonico family.

Black chalk; right half outlined in pen and brown ink. 15 13/16 x 10 7/16 inches (403 x 266 mm.). Watermark: Fleur-de-lis in double circle with mark CB above.

Working drawing with measurements for the panel set between the two obelisks to the right of the central stele in the wall of the piazzale of the Priory of the Order of Malta.

Bibliography: Mayor, 1952, fig. 87; Thomas, 1954, p. 19 and no. 46; Smith, 1961, no. 57, p. 104, pl. 48; *Drawings from New York Collections*, III, 1971, no. 230, repr.; Wilton-Ely, 1976, pp. 218–19, fig. 8; Wilton-Ely, 1978, no. 230, repr.

54. SANTA MARIA AVENTINA: Horizontal panel with trophies and insignia of Rezzonico family.

Pen and brown ink with black chalk underdrawing and also overwork. 8 1/8 x 14 7/8 inches (207 x 379 mm.).

Working drawing with measurements for the decorative panel below the central stele in the wall of the piazzale of the Priory of the Order of Malta.

Bibliography: Mayor, 1952, fig. 89; Thomas, 1954, under no. 46; Wilton-Ely, 1976, pp. 217–18, fig. 6; Wilton-Ely, 1978, no. 229.

55. SAN GIOVANNI IN LATERANO: Longitudinal section through length of nave looking toward the south wall, with proposed scheme for alteration of west end.

Verso: COMPUTATIONS, SMALL PUTTO HEAD.

Pen and brown ink over pencil; brown and gray washes; in left half of drawing, moldings marking horizontal divisions of wall in gray-black ink. Verso, pen and brown ink. 21 x 58 1/4 inches (534 x 1,481 mm.). Three sheets of paper and fraction of another pasted together. Watermark: Fleur-de-lis in double circle with mark CB above. Occurs three times. Inscribed lower

right: Originale del Cav^e. Gio. Batta Piranesi. Probably not Piranesi's hand. Inscribed upper left in pencil in nineteenth-century hand: San Giovanni in Laterano. Also inscribed B.P. as on no. 43.

Reference is made to the project with which this drawing and nos. 56–58 are connected in the foreword of the *Diverse maniere d'adornare i cammini*, 1769, addressed to Cardinal G. B. Rezzonico. Here Piranesi speaks of "L'approvazione, di cui avete onorato, e i disegni impostimi dal Santissimo Padre [Clement XIII] pel compimento della Basilica Lateranense. . . ."

Bibliography: Thomas, 1954, under no. 50; Fischer, 1968, pp. 207–26 (also including discussion of nos. 56–58); Columbia, 1972, discusses nos. 55–58 in relation to Columbia's series of presentation drawings for the projected alteration of the Lateran; Wilton-Ely, 1978, no. 220, repr.

56. SAN GIOVANNI IN LATERANO: Longitudinal section, beginning at transept and showing proposed scheme for alteration of west end of church.

Pen and brown ink, wash, with traces of pencil. 12 9/16 x 21 3/8 inches (320 x 545 mm.). Inscribed on verso: Ponte S. Angelo/Teatro di Marcello/Piramide Nuova/Foro d'Nerva/Curia Ostilia/Tempio di Cibelle/S. Urbano/Foro di Giove(?)/Portico d'Adriano/Interno.

Bibliography: Corfiato, 1951, pl. 62; Thomas, 1954, under no. 50; Smith, 1961, no. 66; *Drawings from New York Collections*, III, 1971, no. 231, repr.; Bacou, 1974, p. 124.

57. SAN GIOVANNI IN LATERANO: Section through choir showing proposed alteration; at right, ground plan of piers with measurements.

Pen and dark brown ink with India-ink washes over pencil. 13 5/8 x 15 1/4 inches (347 x 388 mm.). Watermark: Fleur-de-lis in double circle with mark CB above.

Bibliography: Mayor, 1952, fig. 98; Thomas, 1954, under no. 50.

58. SAN GIOVANNI IN LATERANO: Sketch for choir wall. Putti (opposite direction).

Verso: SKETCH FOR PEDIMENTED NICHE OF CHOIR WALL; PART OF A GROUND PLAN.

Pen and dark brown ink with India-ink wash over pencil. Verso, pencil. 13 11/16 x 10 1/4 inches (349 x 260 mm.). Watermark: Fleur-de-lis in double circle with mark CB above.

Bibliography: Thomas, 1954, no. 50; for verso, Fischer, 1968, p. 212, fig. 9b (part of ground plan of Piranesi's Lateran project, other fragment on verso of no. 110); *Drawings from New York Collections*, III, 1971, no. 232, repr.; Wilton-Ely, 1978, under no. 226.

DECORATIVE

59. DESIGN FOR MANTELPIECE: Masks on lintel and addorsed Victories on jambs.

Verso: fragment of etching after Guercino.

Pen and brown ink with traces of black chalk. 6 1/16 x 11 3/4 inches (155 x 298 mm.).

Study for the etching in *Diverse maniere d'adornare i cammini*, 1769. F. 879.

Bibliography: Rieder, 1973, discussion and concordance of all known drawings related to the *Diverse maniere*, including Morgan nos. 59, 60, 63, 67, 69, 70, 86, 89, 96, 97, 103, 106, 114.

60. SKETCHES FOR MANTELPIECE AND TABLE.

Pen and brown ink; incidental traces of red and black chalk. 11 1/16 (right margin) x 13 3/16 inches (281 x 336 mm.). Inscribed: (at left) Camilli marmi ò cigni; (at right) fronde o teste.

Bibliography: Thomas, 1954, under no. 48; Watson, 1965, p. 102.

61. DESIGN FOR MANTELPIECE WITH CONFRONTED ELEPHANT HEADS. AT LEFT, PILASTER WITH LION HEAD.

Verso: fragment of Ottaviani etching after Guercino.

Pen and brown ink over black chalk. Smudges of red chalk at right. 8 3/8 x 12 11/16 inches (213 x 322 mm.). Inscribed at lower right: rotta de c . . ./carioni(?).

Bibliography: Thomas, 1954, under no. 48; Smith, 1961, no. 68; *Drawings from New York Collections*, III, 1971, no. 234, repr.; Wilton-Ely, 1978, no. 267.

62. DESIGN FOR MANTELPIECE WITH CORNER MEDALLION WITH DOUBLE PORTRAIT HEADS. SKETCH OF SEATED FIGURE.

Verso: fragment of etching, pl. XIV of *Antichità d'Albano e di Castel Gandolfo*, 1764. F. 523.

Pen and brown ink with traces of black chalk. Smudges of red chalk. 6 3/8 x 9 5/8 inches (161 x 246 mm.). Inscribed at left: fiacole.

Bibliography: Smith, 1961, no. 69.

63. DESIGN FOR MANTELPIECE: Wreath in center of lintel: lion paw terminating in head on jambs. At right, traces of sketch of column base.

Verso: FRAGMENTARY SKETCH OF WALL PANEL.

Red chalk, some black chalk with additions in pen and brown ink. Verso, pen and brown ink. 9 1/8 x 14 5/16 inches (232 x 364 mm.).

Study for the etching in *Diverse maniere d'adornare i cammini*, 1769. F. 893.

Bibliography: *Drawings from New York Collections*, III, 1971, no. 235, repr.; Wilton-Ely, 1978, no. 255.

64. DESIGN FOR MANTELPIECE: Bird at base of jamb; satyr head below corner volutes. Separate details of ornament.

Verso: OUTLINE SKETCH OF RECLINING WINGED FIGURE IN ANGLE OF PEDIMENT.

Pen and brown ink with additions in red chalk. 8 x 11 3/8 inches (204 x 289 mm.). Inscribed at right: a miente [miemite?]. Verso: fortuna (repeated five times), not in Piranesi's hand.

65. DESIGN FOR MANTELPIECE: Volutes and dolphins at center of lintel and shell at end; medallion, dolphins, and triangular ornament on jamb.

Verso: fragment of proof impression (before inscription) of etching, pl. XVII from *Antichità d'Albano e di Castel Gandolfo*, 1764. F. 526.

Pen and brown ink over red chalk. 7 15/16 x 14 3/16 inches (202 x 361 mm.).

66. DESIGN FOR MANTELPIECE: Masks on lintel; bird on one jamb, rabbit on other.

Verso: VIEW OF CORNER OF TEMPLE AND ADJACENT BUILDING WITH TILE ROOF. Temple entablature lettered: CASTORI·POLLVCI·DEC·S·FAC/M·CALVIVS·M·F·P·N·

Pen and brown ink over red chalk. Verso, red chalk; traces of black chalk in capital. 7 15/16 x 12 1/4 inches (203 x 311 mm.). Inscribed at lower right: coniglii.

The drawing on the verso is a study for the right corner of the etching "Rovine del Tempio de' Castori nella città di Cora," in *Antichità di Cora* [1764]. F. 541.

67. DESIGN FOR MANTELPIECE: Tablet with frieze and medallion with Wolf of Rome in center of lintel; dog, serpent, and ram head on jamb with border of medallions.

Verso: fragment of etching, pl. VI of *Antichità di Cora* [1764]. F. 546.

Pen and brown ink over black chalk and a few traces of red. 6 15/16 x 12 3/16 inches (176 x 309 mm.). Inscribed at right: medaglie/con Roma de/Cesari, trium/viri, e ditatori.

Study for the etching in *Diverse maniere d'adornare i cammini*, 1769. F. 900.

68. DESIGN FOR MANTELPIECE WITH EGYPTIAN ORNAMENT: Confronted sphinxes at center of lintel; standing figures addorsed to jambs and bird with outspread wings at angle of lintel and jamb.

Verso: fragment of unidentified etching.

Pen and brown ink. 8 9/16 (right margin) x 12 3/16 inches (218 x 309 mm.).

Bibliography: Thomas, 1954, under no. 48; Wilton-Ely, 1978, no. 278.

69. DESIGN FOR MANTELPIECE: Eagle, festoon, and satyr heads at center of lintel; addorsed satyr heads at end.

Verso: FRAGMENT OF GROUND PLAN.

Pen and brown ink with red chalk. Verso, red chalk over black. 8 5/8 (upper margin) x 5 15/16 (right margin) inches (220 x 152 mm.). Inscribed on verso: Pianta dell'Anfiteatro Albano eretto dall'Imp. Domi-[tiano?]/e presentem^te rinchiuso nell' orto de Monaci Gr[egoriani?] S. Paolo Della a. Not in Piranesi's hand.

Study for the etching in *Diverse maniere d'adornare i cammini*, 1769. F. 873.

70. DESIGN FOR MANTELPIECE: Tablet and griffins on lintel; candelabra on jamb.

Verso: fragment of etching, pl. XV of *Le rovine del Castello dell' Acqua Giulia*. F. 416.

Pen and brown ink. 7 11/16 x 6 11/16 (upper margin) inches (196 x 170 mm.).

Study for the etching in *Diverse maniere d'adornare i cammini*, 1769. F. 880.

Bibliography: Berlin Kunstbibliothek, 1975, under no. 886, which was originally part of the same sheet. Nos. 871–899 are all designs for mantelpieces.

71. DESIGNS FOR ORNAMENTAL FRAME AND FOR CARTOUCHE.
Verso: FRAGMENT OF DESIGN FOR TITLE PAGE WITH REMNANT OF TITLE READING: [. . .]ASTEL GANDOLFO/ [. . .] RITTE ED INCISE/DA/[. . .]AMBATISTA [. . .]RANESI.
Pen and brown ink; a few traces of red chalk. Verso, red chalk over black; lettering in pen. 7 1/8 x 10 3/8 inches (180 x 264 mm.).
The drawing on the verso is a fragment of a study for the title page of *Antichità d'Albano e di Castel Gandolfo*, 1764. F. 505.

72. DESIGN FOR MANTELPIECE: Bucranes and festoons on lintel; addorsed satyrs on jamb.
Black chalk. 10 9/16 x 8 1/8 (upper margin) inches (269 x 207 mm.).

73. DESIGN FOR MANTELPIECE: Tablet and festoons in center of lintel with medallion at end.
Verso: FRAGMENTARY SKETCH OF MANTELPIECE.
Pen and brown ink. Verso, black and red chalk. 3 7/16 x 4 13/16 inches (89 x 124 mm.).
This drawing and nos. 74, 75, and 82 appear to be related sketches developing an idea culminating in the design of no. 77.

74. DESIGN FOR MANTELPIECE: Tablet and festoons in center of lintel with medallion at end.
Pen and brown ink. 3 15/16 x 6 (upper margin) inches (100 x 152 mm.).

75. THREE SKETCHES FOR MANTELPIECE: Tablet and festoons in center of lintel with medallion at end.
Verso: PROFILE (?). COMPUTATIONS.
Pen and brown ink. Verso, black and red chalk. 7 1/4 x 12 3/4 inches (185 x 324 mm.).
Bibliography: Thomas, 1954, under no. 48.

76. DESIGN FOR MANTELPIECE: Jamb with volutes.
Pen and brown ink. 3 7/8 x 2 9/16 inches (100 x 66 mm.).

77. DESIGN FOR MANTELPIECE: Tablet in center of lintel linked by festoons to wreaths at either end. At right, separate detail of jamb.
Verso: GUIDE LINES FOR FRAMEWORK OF MANTELPIECE.
Black chalk. 9 5/16 x 16 5/16 inches (238 x 415 mm.). Watermark: Fleur-de-lis in single circle with heart-shaped cartouche surmounted by a cross and enclosing letters AMG above; below letter F.
S
Bibliography: Wilton-Ely, 1978, no. 286 (refers to Morgan no. 85 rather than no. 77).

78. DESIGN FOR MANTELPIECE: Figures of standing Victories above lintel.
Pen and brown ink. 6 1/4 x 5 7/8 inches (159 x 150 mm.). Inscribed on verso: dira che il denaro è corso; imperocchè se io/ve l'ho dato, anche voi dovete dato a me/in pegno la vostra parola d'onore intorno/alla buona qualità de'rami, parola che/ha forza non solamente in quanto vi prema di riscattar/la, ma di far vi stare a ragione/avanti quals.ª giudice e tribunale. Terminerò/anch'io la mia lettera con le stesse parole con cui voi terminate/la vostra: se i rami (voi mi dite) fussero/nello stato in cui/furono consegnati a'vri agenti in Parigi/vi torno a dire, che con buona carta e buoni/ordigni, ed una mano esperta, sarebbero tuttav.ª/capaci ad adempire ad ogni promessa, che/io vi feci a riguardo di essi. Il Sig. Barazz[. . .]/dara costare che i rami sono nello stato in/[che] furono consegnati ai suoi comm.ii in Parigi/[. . .]i rami si torneranno a Parigi, e là con buona/[. . .] e buoni ordigni, ed una mano esperta[. . .]. Not in Piranesi's hand.

79. DESIGN FOR MANTELPIECE: Bucrane, festoons, and medallion with reclining figure on lintel; head of Medusa at end. Sketch of masonry.
Pen and brown ink. 5 15/16 x 6 3/4 inches (150 x 171 mm.). Inscribed on verso, fragment of letter, cut off at right: Piranesi nello stesso temp[ore . . .]/ga' à compatirlo si non le'[. . .]/in persona trovandosi poco [. . .]/é lo prega si lo potesse f[. . .]/àvanti le Sante feste [. . .]/che lei già và, che ne[. . .]/molto di bisogno, che lei g[. . .]/tirà, chi ha' famiglia [. . .]/ della spesa/poi con il Sig Perosini [. . .]/ mediatore, di quell' materia [. . .]/servitù usategli per fare [. . .]/po della statua del Alta[re . . .]/chi scrive si rasegna all [. . .]. Not in Piranesi's hand.

80. DESIGN FOR MANTELPIECE: Animal claw terminating in head on jamb.
Verso: DESIGN FOR MANTELPIECE: Tablet and festoons on lintel; Ionic column on jamb.
Pen and brown ink. 6 1/2 x 6 inches (166 x 152 mm.).
Bibliography: Thomas, 1954, under 48.

81. DESIGN FOR MANTELPIECE: Head of Medusa at center of lintel; standing figure on jamb.
Pen and brown ink over red chalk. 5 7/8 x 7 1/8 inches (150 x 182 mm.). Inscribed: (at top) nastro—medusa/fra le due; (below) [f]iacole—fiacole—baco [Bacco] che tien/canestra cogliendo l'uva.

82. DESIGN FOR MANTELPIECE: Palmette at center of lintel.
Pen and brown ink. 4 13/16 x 5 inches (124 x 129 mm.). Fragment in inscription on verso, cut away on the left margin: [. . .] rio. 3. Esedra architettata come la gran nave/[. . .] che separa il presbiterio della tribuna/[. . .] le per salire al coro de' musici/[. . .] anditori delle reliquie/. . . Atrij architettati come le navi inferiori/[. . . pres]biterio e la tribuna architettata come la gran nave/[. . .] Basilica/[. . .]ici/[. . .] ante al coro, togliandosi quella del. Not Piranesi's hand; an inscription in the same hand which deals with the same subject matter is found on the verso of no. 88.

83. DESIGN FOR MANTELPIECE: Tablet at center of lintel and medallion at end.
Pen and brown ink. 4 11/16 x 6 9/16 (top) inches (120 x 166 mm.).

84. DESIGN FOR MANTELPIECE: Vase between volutes at center of lintel; animal form on jamb.
Pen and dark brown ink. 7 13/16 x 16 9/16 inches (199 x 422 mm.). Inscribed above lintel: marmo bianco—spugna/paragone nero; (on lintel) porfido

(twice); (on jamb) porfido; (at right) profil[e]/
nati(?). Letters N and B also occur on lintel,
presumably as abbreviations for *nero* and *bianco*.
On the verso is an inscription (cut away slightly on the
margins) dealing with Etruscan vases. It appears to be
notes for the text of the *Diverse maniere d'adornare i
cammini*, 1769, and reads as follows:
[. . .] che addornano i Vasi etrusche si denno
plani(?) proposto alle loro Conoscence
cioe *ornamento secondo* ornamenti

          B   C   E

[m]eandri di piu specie fabrice fustarelli con
   erb[ette]
[t]empieti *G. ed altri intreci in gran copia*
   Pinee H Fonghi I Cocie di pigna
[. . . se]conda clace
[f]igure di tutte specie animali maschere etc.
alle Tavole etc. Queste sono *dell* di quelle
[n]oi fino ad ora riconosciamo per monumenti de
   greci
[. . .] scolpire le cornici e cosi piamente *detti da
   Plinio*
[. . .]ce fiori intagli se *loro templi e cosi se vede*
[. . .] gli Etrusche e ne loro timpani e ne loro
   Frontespici
[ne]l Tempio antichissimo di Giove Capitolino
   che si vedeva ne
   dunque
[. . .] ici. Io non so vedere *cos* ornamenti piu di
   elleganti
[. . .] quie parti galenterie ed anche mosse, come
   io vegg[o]
[. . .] tà de Vasi Etruschi, e nelle architetture
che si vegono per la Toscana. Si dira che alcune
sono tropo bene disegnate per essere cose etrusche
   sopra que vasi
fatte dipinte da Greci e *che* le Piture cative
sono Etrusche le buone sono de greci ma però
[. . .]da quanto habiamo detto *che* stabilindo *che
   che quel*
Vasi egli inventori di questa sorte di com'ne di
[. . .]Toscani da quali Vasi noi abbiamo stabilito
[E]trusco e tutti quelli che fanno in . . . faranno
         tutto lontano del resto
il far Cinecse e un gusto Gofo mal
gonfio a parte dalle maniere ben intese
nel contorno delle fig^re e cosi ne suoi ornamenti
[. . .]sto cio *se* quelle che devono dipingere all'
   etrusca
[d]ipingere le figure *dell'* ultim con buoni cont . . .
[. . .]ffeso ad essere all' etrusca. Ma volte ad una
   perfezione
[. . .]ca e per conseguenza non dobiamo rico-
   noscere pure il
[. . .]l Vaso etrusco. Dunque se si pensa a dese . . .
ci constano che i Toscani erano avedutissimi (?)
   nella
perfezione e ce lo attesta pplinio non ve de . . . che
[s]ia Toscano et eccellente ancora la stattua de
   Medici è
[. . .]e . . . in Roma che si vegono *ad* ancora *con*
   uno
         che
[. . .] quelli io *ne* pongo *uno* . . .

85. DESIGN FOR MANTELPIECE: Relief with six figures at
center of lintel and sea deities at either end; foliate
ornament with Minerva and bucrane on jambs.
   Pen and brown ink over black chalk. 9 11/16 x 13 3/8
inches (246 x 340 mm.). Measurements and scale indicated.
   Bibliography: Rieder, 1975, p. 585, fig. 17; also discussion of Morgan nos. 73–75, 77, 82, 83; Wilton-Ely,
1978, no. 286 (the author incorrectly refers to this
drawing as Morgan no. 77).

86. DESIGN FOR MANTELPIECE AND CHAIR.
   Pen and brown ink over preliminary outlines in black
chalk. 7 1/8 x 13 15/16 inches (182 x 354 mm.)
Inscribed at left: . . . scudo (?).
   Bibliography: Mayor, 1952, fig. 112; Scott, 1975, p.
225, fig. 260.

87. SKETCH FOR MANTELPIECE: Tablet and ram heads on
lintel; alternate scheme of palmette frieze.
   Pen and brown ink. 5 3/4 x 7 1/2 inches (147 x 192
mm.). Watermark: Six-pointed star in a circle with
cross above and letter F below.

88. DESIGN FOR MANTELPIECE: Lintel terminating in volutes; acanthus leaf at base of jamb with wreath sus-
pended from bar above.
   Pen and brown ink over red chalk. 5 13/16 x 5 1/16
inches (148 x 129 mm.). Fragment of inscription on
verso, cut away at top and at left margin; in same hand
and dealing with same subject as 82:
[. . .]infamia, *riferiscono* asseriscono soltanto
[. . .]Presbiterio elevato due gradi di piu' dell' Esedra
[. . .]Esedra al pari della crociata
[. . .]Coro de Musici.
[. . .]Scale per salire al coro de'Musici
[. . .]Scale per salire ai conditori delle reliquie
[. . .]Ambulacro *che si corre dietro al* ora La Tribuna
   e'L Presbiterio
[. . .]Porte deretane della Basilica
[. . .]Porta della Sagrestia
[. . .]Tribuna. 2. Presbiterio. 3. Esedra
[. . . co]lonnato, o sia *st*, steccatore separa
[. . . st]*eccate di colonne che ristringe*, il Presbiterio
   dentro, dalla
[. . .]Tribuna. 5. ambulacro fra La Tribuna e 'L Pres-
   bi[terio]
     [. . .]ro de'Musici. 6. Scale per salire.

89. SKETCH FOR MANTELPIECE: Lion head and leg on inner
side of jamb.
   VERSO: ORNAMENT.
   Pen, and black and red chalk. Verso, black chalk. 10
x 7 3/16 (upper margin) inches (255 x 182 mm.).
   Preliminary sketch for etching in *Diverse maniere
d'adornare i cammini*, 1769. F. 883.

90. SKETCH FOR MANTELPIECE: Candelabra on jamb.
   Pen and brown ink. 4 x 3 9/16 inches (102 x 91
mm.). Fragment of draft of letter on verso, cut away on
all margins; not in Piranesi's hand:
[. . .]averne *fra* alla [. . .]
[. . .]*Inghilterra La* G. Brettagne che dalle altre [. . .]
[. . .]lla si persuadera' facilmente, che il mio att . . . ma
   [. . .]

[. . .]ia per *colere* gl' Inglesi che professario ed aman [. . .]

[. . .]bi, *or Giudici Ella se qualunque volta* [. . .]

[. . .]*occasione di trattare con esselere, e di* [. . .]

[. . .]*ai nostri communi studi io possa sia*

[. . .] Or fra *questi pattrioti ha* gli altri avendo La consolazione[. . .]

[. . .]erne due ne' di Lei Sig^ri Figli, *i quali* [. . .]

[. . .]n *giudi* dovra maraviglarsi [. . .] i quali co[. . .]

[. . .]enti L'uno nella pittura e L'altro ne [. . .]

[. . .]cominciano ad essere L'ornamento della [. . .]

[. . .]*he voluto*

[. . .]lina non dovra' maravigliarsi se[. . .]

91. SKETCH FOR MANTELPIECE: Tablets in center of lintel; gaine on jamb at right.

Pen and brown ink with traces of red chalk. 2 3/4 x 4 11/16 inches (70 x 120 mm.). Fragment of price list on verso; not in Piranesi's hand:

. . . de Cora pro(?)	64
Academia di Francia pro:	54(?)
Piazza di S. Pietro pro: 120	
Piazza Navona pro: (?) 120	
	3.

92. SKETCHES FOR MANTELPIECES AND CANDELABRA.

Verso: fragment of printed map of Northern Italy.

Pen and brown ink; fragmentary sketch of ornament in black chalk. 17 1/4 x 25 1/8 inches (439 x 638 mm.). Computations along right margin. Inscribed: (at top) alabastro/marmo/alabastro/porfido/—camino . . .—due compagni—gola—medusa; (at bottom) B bianco—a porfido—medusa—cigno—cerrula(?).

Bibliography: Thomas, 1954, under no. 48.

93. TWO SKETCHES FOR CANDELABRA.

Pen and brown ink; few lines in red chalk at bottom. 8 3/8 x 1 11/16 inches (213 x 43 mm.).

94. SKETCHES FOR ORNAMENT (SHIELDS?).

Pen and brown ink. 5 9/16 x 5 1/16 inches (141 x 130 mm.). Inscribed on verso: ECTIAIA.

95. SKETCHES FOR CANDELABRA.

Pen and brown ink. 8 3/16 x 5 3/16 inches (207 x 132 mm.).

96. DESIGNS FOR SEDAN CHAIR AND COACH.

Verso: fragment of etching from the *Diverse maniere d'adornare i cammini*, 1769. F. 862.

Red chalk (lower design); pen and brown ink (upper design). 11 11/16 x 5 3/16 inches (297 x 132 mm.)

The drawing of the coach with the decoration of alternating winged figures and rosettes is a study for the etched design in *Diverse maniere d'adornare i cammini*, 1769. F. 922. The other drawing appears to be a first idea for the etched design of the sedan chair with the circular window divided by a foliate molding and with a circular panel below. F. 921.

Bibliography: Thomas, 1954, under no. 48; Berlin Kunstbibliothek, 1975, under no. 898.

97. DESIGN FOR COACH.

Verso: fragment of etching from the *Diverse maniere d'adornare i cammini*, 1769. F. 890.

Pen and brown ink; two extraneous cross marks in red chalk. 5 1/8 x 5 7/16 inches (131 x 138 mm.).

An early and probably discarded sketch (as indicated by the red lines crossing the face of the drawing) for the etched design of the coach with the triple opening and trophy finials in the *Diverse maniere d'adornare i cammini*, 1769. F. 920. The etching differs in several respects from the sketch but the basic design is retained.

Bibliography: Thomas, 1954, pp. 19–20 and no. 48; Wilton-Ely, 1978, no. 260a.

98. DESIGNS FOR COACH AND SEDAN CHAIR: At left, coach with triple opening and circular paneling; at right, chair with ivy ornament and goat finials.

Verso: fragment of etching from the *Diverse maniere d'adornare i cammini*, 1769. F. 862.

Pen and brown ink over red chalk (left design); red chalk (right design). 4 7/8 x 8 3/8 inches (125 x 213 mm.). Inscribed: farfal[la?].

Both drawings are studies for the etched designs in *Diverse maniere d'adornare i cammini*, 1769. F. 922.

Bibliography: Mayor, 1952, fig. 109; Thomas, 1954, under no. 48; Wilton-Ely, 1978, no. 260b.

99. SKETCHES FOR DECORATION OF BODIES OF COACHES.

Verso: fragment of etching from the *Diverse maniere d'adornare i cammini*, 1769. F. 909.

Pen and brown ink. 9 1/8 x 14 3/4 inches (232 x 376 mm.). Inscribed: bianco-roso con figure bianche/picole.

Bibliography: Thomas, 1954, under no. 48.

100. SKETCHES FOR DECORATION OF BODIES OF COACHES.

Verso: fragment of etching from the *Diverse maniere d'adornare i cammini*, 1769. F. 909.

Pen and brown ink; few spiraling strokes in black chalk. 9 1/16 x 13 9/16 inches (231 x 345 mm.). Inscribed at left: festoni bianchi mero oro — roso — nero — colori — bianco — verde — gialo/alabastro/sangui[gna]; at right, gialo — alabastro gi[. . .] bianco — verde a — a nero/ornamenti bianc[hi].

Bibliography: Thomas, 1954, under no. 48.

101. SKETCH FOR ORNAMENT WITH GRIFFIN ON BASE.

Red chalk. 3 11/16 x 2 5/16 inches (95 x 60 mm.). Watermark (fragmentary): Medallion and section of double chain.

102. CHAIR WITH SHIELD BACK.

Pen and brown ink; extraneous strokes in black chalk. 3 1/16 x 1 13/16 inches (78 x 47 mm.). Watermark: Indecipherable fragment. Inscription on verso: Nine Inches hig[h]/five Inches hi[gh]. Not in Piranesi's hand.

The presence of the inscription in English is puzzling. Stylistically, the drawing appears acceptable.

103. DESIGN FOR CLOCK.

Red chalk over black. 4 1/2 x 2 7/16 inches (115 x 62 mm.).

Preliminary sketch for clock at left of etched plate labeled "Quest' orologio A e stato eseguito in

metallo/dorato per ordine di Sua Ecceza il Sig^r/D. Abondio Rezzonico Senatore di Roma,/come ancora alcuni altri ornam'ti che si vedono sparsi nelle altre tavole di questa/raccolta quali sono stati messi in opera/nel sui Palazzo sul Campidoglio," *Diverse maniere d'adornare i cammini*, 1769. F. 924.
  Bibliography: Wilton-Ely, 1978, no. 265a.

104. DESIGN FOR STOOL.
  Pen and brown ink over black chalk. 2 13/16 x 4 5/16 inches (71 x 111 mm.).

105. ORNAMENT WITH INTERTWINED DOLPHINS.
  Pen and brown ink. 2 1/8 x 2 3/16 inches (54 x 55 mm.).

106. THREE SCONCES.
  Verso: COVER FOR VASE: Knob in leaf design; strigil border.
  Red chalk over black. Verso, black chalk. 9 3/16 x 5 3/16 inches (234 x 132 mm.).
  The two-branched sconce at the right is a preparatory sketch for the etched design at the upper left of pl. 63 of *Diverse maniere d'adornare i cammini*, 1769. F. 923.
  Bibliography: Thomas, 1954, pp. 19–20, no. 49, also under no. 48; Bacou, 1974, p. 132; Wilton-Ely, 1978, no. 265b, repr.

107. DESIGN FOR OVAL MIRROR FRAME: Festoons and winged *putto* heads.
  Pen and brown ink with India-ink washes over pencil. 18 9/16 x 13 1/2 inches (472 x 344 mm.). Watermark: Fleur-de-lis in double circle with mark CB below.
  Bibliography: Thomas, 1954, p. 19 and under no. 47; Wilton-Ely, 1978, under no. 269.

108. DESIGN FOR OVAL MIRROR FRAME: Floral ornament.
  Pen and brown ink with India-ink wash over pencil. 18 3/8 x 13 1/2 inches (468 x 345 mm.).
  Bibliography: Thomas, 1954, no. 47; Wilton-Ely, 1978, under no. 269.

109. DESIGN FOR RECTANGULAR FRAME FOR OVAL MIRROR: Floral ornament with dove in wreath at top, winged *putto* heads at sides and bottom.
  Pen and brown ink with India-ink wash over pencil. 19 11/16 x 15 3/16 inches (501 x 386 mm.).
  Bibliography: Mayor, 1952, fig. 114; Thomas, 1954, under no. 47; Wilton-Ely, 1978, no. 269.

Miscellaneous

110. DESIGN FOR WALL MONUMENT WITH PAPAL AND DUCAL CROWNS: Oval frame for portrait(?).
  Verso: FRAGMENT OF GROUND PLAN FOR SAN GIOVANNI IN LATERANO.
  Pen and brown ink with India-ink wash over preliminary outlines in black chalk. Verso, black chalk. 13 3/16 x 7 3/16 inches (336 x 182 mm.).
  Bibliography: Fischer, 1968, p. 212, figs. 8a and 9a (originally part of same sheet as no. 58); *Drawings from*

New York Collections, III, 1971, no. 233, repr.; Wilton-Ely, 1978, no. 226.

111. PAPAL CARTOUCHE WITH TIARA AND KEYS.
  Pen and brown ink. 10 1/8 x 5 7/8 inches (258 x 150 mm.).

112. FOUNTAIN: Upper basin topped by pineapple and supported by sphinxes; dolphin spouts emptying into lower basin.
  Verso: ORNAMENT (fragmentary).
  Black chalk. 9 3/4 x 5 5/16 inches (248 x 136 mm.).

113. VASE(?) WITH FIGURE OF VICTORY.
  Verso: CORNICE. COMPUTATIONS.
  Pen and brown ink. Verso, black chalk; several numbers in red chalk. 8 9/16 x 3 15/16 inches (218 x 100 mm.).

114. TABERNACLE.
  Verso: DESIGNS FOR TWO CHAIRS (fragmentary).
  Pen and black-brown ink over black chalk; verso, pen and brown ink. 5 5/16 x 3 3/4 inches (135 x 95 mm.).
  The chair at the left on the verso is a sketch for the etched design at the bottom of pl. 66 of *Diverse maniere d'adornare i cammini*, 1769. F. 926.

115. PERSPECTIVE SKETCH FOR DECORATIVE PANEL: Circular pattern of medallions and garlands.
  Pen and brown ink over red chalk. 9 7/8 x 8 7/8 inches (255 x 232 mm.). Inscribed: Pa^{mi} 124 1/4.

116. SKETCH OF FIGURE, VASES, AND ?
  Pen and brown ink. 6 x 10 inches (153 x 254 mm.). Inscribed: Vaso Ville Medici. Verso, list of Piranesi publications in clerical hand; right margin cut.
  Antichità Romane in Quattro Tomi al prezzo di Quindici Zecchini . . . .
    Legatura de' Sud^i . . . .
  Della Magnificenza de Romani in un Tomo al prezzo [di] Cinque Zecchini . . . .
  Risposta di Mosiu Mariette . . . .
    Legatura del Sud^o . . . .
  Il Campo Marzo in un Tomo al prezzo di Quattro Zecchini . . . .
    Legatura del Sud^o . . . .
  L'Antichità d'Albano in un Tomo al prezzo di Quattro [Zec] chini e mezzo . . . .
    Legatura del Sud^o . . . .
  Vedute di Roma in due Tomi Num^o. al prezzo d[i] bajocchi 25: L'una . . . .
  Pianta di Roma inclusa nel p.mo Tomo . . . .
    Legatura de' Sud^i . . . .
  Vasi, e candelabri in un Tomo num^o. al prezzo di [ba]-jocchi 25: L'uno . . . .
    Legatura del Sud^o . . . .
  Colonna Trajana in un Tomo al prezzo di Quattro Zecc[hini] e mezzo . . . .
    Legatura del Sud^o . . . .
  Opere varie in un Tomo al prezzo di . . . .
  Carceri d'invenzione un Tomo al prezzo di . . . .
  Trofei d'Ottaviano Augusto un Tomo al prezzo di . . . .

Archi antichi in un Tomo al prezzo di . . . .
     Legatura de' Sud^i . . . .
Antichità di Cora un Tomo al prezzo di . . . .
Trattato del castello del Acqua Giulia un Tomo . . . . . .
Raccolta de disegni del Guercino . . . .
     Legatura de' Sud^i . . . .
Le due Stampe di Dorigny . . . .
L'Opera del Signor Hamilton . . . .
     Legatura del Sud^o . . . .
Fasti Consolari un Tomo al prezzo di . . . .

This sketch and nos. 117–119 are apparently related. They are little more than shorthand notations that elude satisfactory identification. The prices given in the inscription on the verso coincide with those listed in Piranesi's engraved catalogue of his own works with the exception that in the engraved catalogue the prices of the *Vedute di Roma* and of the *Vasi, e candelabri* are given in *paoli* instead of *bajocchi*.

117. SKETCH OF HEAD AND SHOULDERS OF MAN.
  Pen and brown ink. 3 3/16 x 3 1/8 inches (82 x 80 mm.).

118. SKETCH OF SEATED NUDE MALE FIGURE. (In opposite direction) SKETCH OF BALUSTRADE, VASE, COLUMN, WINGED FIGURE, etc.
  Pen and brown ink. 10 13/16 x 8 inches (275 x 200 mm.). Inscribed at lower right: Plani. . . .

119. SKETCH OF BALUSTRADE, COLUMN, GARLAND.
  Verso: SKETCH OF BALUSTRADE, CORNUCOPIA (?).
  Pen and brown ink. 5 x 10 1/4 inches (128 x 261 mm.). Watermark: Six-pointed star in a circle with cross above and letter F below. Inscribed: (at left) giocoliere; (at right) piante. Verso: due cornucopi.

120. SKETCH FOR PROW OF SHIP (?).
  Pen and brown ink. 5 7/8 x 8 1/8 inches (149 x 208 mm.).
  Bibliography: Thomas, 1954, under no. 16.

121. CARTOUCHE.
  Pen and brown ink with traces of red chalk. 2 3/4 x 5 3/16 inches (71 x 132 mm.). Lettering in center of cartouche has been effaced and only letters ESSATO are now decipherable.

122. SKETCHES OF HEAD AND SHOULDERS OF BEARDED MAN.
  Pen and brown ink. 6 3/8 x 5 1/2 inches (163 x 140 mm.). Inscribed on verso: (Fragment of account which cannot be fully deciphered as drawing has been backed).

123. SKETCHES OF ORNAMENT.
  Verso: SKETCHES OF ORNAMENT.
  Black chalk. 8 5/16 x 11 inches (211 x 279 mm.). Watermark (fragmentary): Part of cartouche with word FABRIANO. Inscribed upper left: Lume di metallo/S. Lorenzo alla strada—alla Salita Monte Ollivetto/Carlini/g. Verso: (left) . . .; (right) gros[s]o a piu—spado—meno.

The following drawings (124–133) are not fully convincing as being by Piranesi's own hand and may be the work of pupils or assistants.

124. VASE: Masks and bird heads on handles; in central register, three nude figures bowing before bird in a temple.
  Pen and India-ink wash. 8 5/16 x 4 13/16 inches (212 x 123 mm.). Watermark: Indecipherable fragment.
  An outline sketch of the same vase appears at the lower left on the sheet of sketches, no. 17. The present drawing, however, lacks the surety of Piranesi's own hand. No. 125 is executed in similar style.

125. VASE: Serpentine handles encircling body; four dancing nudes on neck.
  Pen and India-ink wash. 7 11/16 x 6 3/8 inches (196 x 163 mm.).

126. DESIGN FOR BOOKPLATE FOR CARDINAL OF ALBANI FAMILY: Cartouche with Albani arms (a fess between a molet of eight points in chief, and a triple mount in base) surmounted by cardinal's hat and set against shell; bearded grotesque at bottom.
  Pen and brown ink with India-ink wash. 4 11/16 x 3 3/4 inches (121 x 96 mm.).

127. DESIGN FOR BOOKPLATE FOR CARDINAL OF ALBANI FAMILY: Cartouche with Albani arms surmounted by cardinal's hat and supported by two angels with trumpets.
  Verso: FRAGMENT OF DESIGN FOR CARDINAL'S ARMS: Cartouche with lion rampant surmounted by cardinal's hat and set over Maltese cross.
  Pen and brown ink with India-ink wash. Verso, black chalk with yellow-gray wash. 4 13/16 x 4 1/4 (upper margin) inches (123 x 109 mm.).

128. STUDY OF STATUE OF DRAPED SEATED FEMALE FIGURE HOLDING A SERPENT.
  Pen and India-ink with buff and brown washes. 9 5/16 x 6 1/4 inches (237 x 165 mm.). Inscribed upper right corner: Gustinian. Not Piranesi's hand.

129. STUDY AFTER STATUE OF DRAPED STANDING FEMALE FIGURE HOLDING A WREATH IN HER LEFT HAND.
  Pen and brown ink. 8 3/4 x 6 1/16 inches (223 x 154 mm.). Watermark: (Fragmentary) Grapes (?). Inscribed upper right: Gustinian. Not Piranesi's hand.

130. STUDY AFTER STATUE OF STANDING YOUTH.
  Pen and brown ink. 7 1/2 x 6 1/4 inches (191 x 160 mm.). Watermark: (Fragmentary) Part of ivy leaf (?). Inscribed upper right: Ancelotti (?). Not Piranesi's hand.

131. SKETCH OF HADRIANIC MEDALLION FROM THE ARCH OF CONSTANTINE.
  Verso: STANDING FIGURE IN TOGA.
  Pencil; faint trace of red chalk in border of medallion. 4 1/4 x 5 3/16 inches (110 x 132 mm.).
  Bibliography: Smith, 1961, no. 20.

132. MEDLEY OF CLASSICAL FRAGMENTS: Figure with book and skeleton at his feet in foreground.

Pen and brown ink. 15 5/16 x 18 15/16 inches (390 x 480 mm.).

This drawing, which is apparently a preparatory study for an etching or engraving, is a variant of a drawing in the Louvre (No. 3785) which is attributed to Piranesi.

133. PUTTI WITH HELMET AND TROPHIES.

Pen and brown ink washed. 5 11/16 x 7 7/16 inches (144 x 189 mm.).

Not by Piranesi; seventeenth-century drawing.

PART TWO: Additions to the Collection

A-1. ARCHITECTURAL FANTASY: Diagonal perspective of a colossal arcaded façade fronting on a long piazza with the Horse Tamers and other statues, victory columns, fountains, and an obelisk.

Pen and brown ink, brown wash, some graphite; perspective lines and a few details in red chalk. Irregularly trimmed along lower edge and then made up by the artist and worked in a bolder manner; old vertical crease at center. 10 9/16 x 16 7/8 inches (270 x 428 mm.). Watermark: Illegible design within double circle.

Provenance: purchased from P. and D. Colnaghi, London, 1966.

Bibliography: *Exhibition of Old Master Drawings*, P. and D. Colnaghi, London, 1966, no. 21, repr.; Morgan Library, *Sixteenth Fellows Report*, 1973, p. 119; Wilton-Ely, 1978, no. 41, repr.

Acc. no. 1971.4.
Purchased as the Gift of Miss Alice Tully.

A-2. CENTRAL VIEW OF A CHURCH INTERIOR.

Pen and brown ink, gray and brown wash, over black chalk, with revisions by the artist in pen and darker brown ink and wash, also red chalk. 7 3/8 x 9 11/16 inches (187 x 246 mm.). Watermark: None visible through lining. Inscribed in brown ink by the artist across the architrave: IMPERATOR/JOANES BTTA PIRANESIS/SEPULCRUM EREXIT, signed at lower right: Piranesi.

Provenance: Edmond Fatio (sale, Nicolas Rauch, Geneva, 3–4 June 1959, no. 203).

Bibliography: Morgan Library, *Tenth Fellows Report*, 1960, pp. 59–61; Fischer, 1968, pp. 222–23, fig. 14; Erichsen, 1976, p. 215, fig. 5; Wilton-Ely, 1978, no. 33.

Acc. no. 1959.14.
Purchased as the Gift of the Fellows.

A-3. ASSASSINATION SCENE.

Pen and brown ink, brown wash, over preliminary indications in red chalk; several accidental spots of green watercolor. 9 9/16 x 7 5/16 inches (241 x 185 mm.). Watermark: Six-pointed star within circle (close to no. 3883 in Edward Heawood, *Watermarks, Mainly of the 17th and 18th Centuries*, Hilversum, Holland, 1950). Signed (?) in pen and brown ink at lower left, party on the mount and partly on the drawing: Piranesi. Inscribed in pen and brown ink on verso at lower left: B. P. L. N.º 116; (at center) 15.

Provenance: H. M. Calmann, London, 1951; John S. Newberry, New York; sale, Parke Bernet, New York, 30 March 1961, no. 4; Mr. and Mrs. Eugene V. Thaw, New York.

Bibliography: K. T. Parker, *Catalogue of the Collection of Drawings in the Ashmolean Museum*, II, Oxford, 1956, under no. 1038; Morgan Library, *Sixteenth Fellows Report*, 1973, p. 119; *Drawings from the Collection of Mr. & Mrs. Eugene V. Thaw*, exhibition catalogue by Felice Stampfle & Cara D. Denison with an introduction by Eugene V. Thaw, The Pierpont Morgan Library, New York, 1975, no. 54, repr.

Acc. no. 1968.13.
Gift of Mr. and Mrs. Eugene V. Thaw.

A-4. ARCHITECTURAL FANTASY.

Pen and brown ink, brown wash. 12 15/16 x 9 5/16 inches (329 x 491 mm.). Watermark: None.

Provenance: Janos Scholz, New York (Lugt S. 2933b).

Bibliography: G. Freedley, *Theatrical Designs*, I, New York, 1940, pl. 9; Charles de Tolnay, *History and Techniques of Old Master Drawings*, New York, 1943, no. 142, repr.; Hans Tietze, *European Master Drawings in the United States*, New York, 1947, p. 202, pl. 101; Janos Scholz, *Baroque and Romantic Stage Design*, New York, 1949, p. 14, pl. 68; Mayor, 1952, p. 38, pl. 24; Smith, 1961, no. 24; *Italian Drawings from the Collection of Janos Scholz*, Arts Council, London, 1968, no. 71, pl. 24; *Drawings from New York Collections*, III, 1971, no. 226, repr.; Morgan Library, *Seventeenth Fellows Report*, 1976, p. 176, pl. 17; Wilton-Ely, 1978, no. 45.

Acc. no. 1974.27.
Gift of Mr. Janos Scholz.

A-5. SANTA MARIA AVENTINA (also called SANTA MARIA DEL PRIORATO): Sketch for the high altar.

Pen and brown ink. 4 5/8 x 4 9/16 inches (118 x 117 mm.). Watermark: None.

Provenance: Purchased from Walter Schatzki, New York, 1952.

Bibliography: Mayor, 1952, p. 18, pl. 81; Morgan Library, *Fourth Fellows Report*, 1953, p. 65; Thomas, 1954, p. 51 under no. 46; Smith, 1961, p. 104, no. 58, pl. 49; Fischer, 1968, pp. 208–09, fig. 4; *Drawings from New York Collections*, III, 1971, no. 228, repr.; Wilton-Ely, 1976, p. 220, fig. 17; Wilton-Ely, 1978, no. 231.

Acc. no. 1952.26.

A-6. RUINS AT POZZUOLI.

Pen and brown-black ink, over black chalk, on a

heavy light brown paper. 19 5/16 x 30 inches (490 x 760 mm.). Creased at the center. Watermark: Animal inscribed in a circle, the letters R U S S below. Inscribed at lower left margin in pen and gray-black ink, the letter P in a rough cartouche; fragment of a somewhat similar inscription on verso.

Provenance: Purchased from H. M. Calmann, London, 1961.

Bibliography: Morgan Library, *Eleventh Fellows Report*, 1961, pp. 93–95, repr. (as "Ruins of Pompeii"); Morgan Library, *Thirteenth Fellows Report*, 1964, p. 103; *Drawings from New York Collections*, III, no. 236, repr.; *The Age of Neo-Classicism*, London, Royal Academy of Arts and Victoria & Albert Museum, and Osterley Park House, 1972, no. 728; Wilton-Ely, 1978, no. 320.

Acc. no. 1961.1.
Purchased as the Gift of the Fellows.

A-7. TEMPLE OF ISIS AT POMPEII.
Reed and quill pens and brown-black ink over preliminary indications in black chalk. 20 1/2 x 30 3/4 inches (520 x 780 mm.). Watermark: Fragment of coat-of-arms surmounted by letter W. Numbered in brown ink from 1 to 20. Inscribed variously; in pen and gray-black ink at lower right: Vedute di due ale dell'atrio del Tenysio [*sic*] d'Iside; on verso in pen and brown-black ink: (at lower right) Vedute di due ale dell'atrio del Tempio d'Iside; (at upper center) 19; (at lower left corner) Part 2ª Rª/ Tav. 120.

Provenance: sale, London, Christie's, 29 June 1962, no. 41, repr.

Bibliography: Morgan Library, *Thirteenth Fellows Report*, 1964, pp. 103ff.; *Neo-classicism: Style and Motif*, The Cleveland Museum of Art, Cleveland, 1964, no. 13, repr.; *The Pierpont Morgan Library: A Review of Acquisitions 1949–1968*, New York, 1969, p. 160, pl. 42; *The Age of Neo-Classicism*, London, Royal Academy of Arts and Victoria & Albert Museum, and Osterley Park House, 1972, no. 729; *Pompeii as Source and Inspiration*, The University of Michigan Museum of Art, Ann Arbor, 1977, no. 35, repr.

Acc. no. 1963.12.
Gift of Mr. Martin L. Levy.

A-8. THREE FIGURES AND ARCHITECTURAL DETAILS.
Verso: Etching pl. xxv of vol. IV of *Le antichità romane*, 1756. F. 360.
Pen and brown-black ink (figures); red and black chalk. 16 9/16 x 21 5/8 inches (420 x 548 mm.). Watermark: Fleur-de-lis in a double circle. Inscribed by the artist: at upper right in red chalk, Segue/a mediano (?)/B/Presbiterio; arco di tran . . ./ primo ordine B arciprete/ di(?) mezzo; at left in opposite direction, dentell/ quadre; in black chalk, lo stesso (?)/ servizio(?) volute le finestre/ pianta/ portone / dalla parte d mezzo della/ faciata/ Campanile (?). Numbered at upper center in black chalk or graphite: 248.

Provenance: L. H. Philippi; purchased from H. M. Calmann, London, 1950.

Bibliography: Morgan Library, *First Fellows Report*, 1950, p. 53.

Acc. no. 1950.9.
Purchased as the Gift of the Fellows.

A-9. FIGURE STUDIES.
Pen and brown ink. 9 1/16 x 5 1/2 inches (230 x 140 mm.). Watermark: Illegible design within circle.

Provenance: J. A. Duval le Camus, Paris (Lugt 1441); Janos Scholz, New York.

Bibliography: Mayor, 1952, p. 39, pl. 41; Thomas, 1954, no. 70, repr.; "Italian Drawings from the Collection of Janos Scholz," *Metropolitan Museum of Art Bulletin*, 1965, part II, p. 343, repr.; *Italian Drawings from the Collection of Janos Scholz*, Arts Council, London, 1968, no. 72; *Drawings from New York Collections*, III, 1971, no. 237, repr.; Wilton-Ely, 1978, no. 108.

Acc. no. 1976.34.
Gift of Mr. Janos Scholz.

A-10. STANDING MAN GESTURING WITH HIS RIGHT ARM.
Black chalk. 5 3/16 x 3 1/4 inches (132 x 82 mm.). Watermark: None.

Provenance: Robert von Hirsch, Basel; Richard S. Davis, Wayzata, Minn.

Bibliography: Morgan Library, *Ninth Fellows Report*, 1959, p. 102.

Acc. no. 1958.6.
Gift of Mr. Richard S. Davis.

A-11. TEMPLE OF ISIS AT POMPEII.
Quill and reed pen in black and some brown ink, black wash, over black chalk; perspective lines and squaring in graphite; several accidental oil stains. Sight measurements 20 1/8 x 30 inches (510 x 760 mm.). Inscribed on verso at lower right in pen and brown ink: Veduta in angolo del tempio d'Isibe [*sic*]. Numerical notations from 1 through 23, in a different brown ink, within the drawing.

Provenance: H. M. Calmann, London; George Ortiz, Geneva; Sydney J. Lamon, New York; sale, London, Christie's, 27 November 1973, no. 314; R. M. Light and Company, Inc., Boston.

Bibliography: *Drawings from the Collection of Mr. & Mrs. Eugene V. Thaw*, exhibition catalogue by Felice Stampfle & Cara D. Denison with an introduction by Eugene V. Thaw, The Pierpont Morgan Library, New York, and elsewhere, 1975–76, no. 56, repr.

Promised Gift of Mr. and Mrs. Eugene V. Thaw.

A-12. DOMED CHURCH, OBELISK AT LEFT.
Verso: DETAIL OF BRACKET.
Pen and brown ink, brown wash, over black chalk; a few extraneous lines in red chalk. Verso, red chalk. 4 3/8 x 7 inches (112 x 178 mm.). Inscribed on verso in pen and brown ink, at upper left: Sig^Re; below is fragment of a document or letter in a notarial hand, cut off at left and right margins; it reads: . . . di Nostro Signore per il canale di VS.llma . . ./ . . . 'accordare a Gio Batista Piranesi, Orator . . ./ . . . one della Gabella dovuta alla Dogana . . ./ . . . carta papale, delle quali egli ha bisogno . . ./ . . . op [obliterated] lle antichità Romane [obliterated] a . . ./ . . . e no gi [obliterated] venuta in Doga [obliterated] . . ./ . . . sieno cinque Le quali dal. . . .

Provenance: Walter Schatzki, New York; Austin A. Mitchell, New York; Mathias Komor, New York.

Bibliography: Mayor, 1952, pp. 18, 33, 40, no. 85, repr.; *Drawings from the Collection of Mr. & Mrs. Eugene V. Thaw,* exhibition catalogue by Felice Stampfle & Cara D. Denison with an introduction by Eugene V. Thaw, The Pierpont Morgan Library, New York, and elsewhere, 1975–76, no. 55, repr.; to be published in *Master Drawings* shortly [as of 1978].

Promised Gift of Mr. and Mrs. Eugene V. Thaw.

THE DRAWINGS

The illustration numbers correspond to the catalogue entries, which have been familiar to scholars since 1948. All the entries are illustrated, but exigencies of page layout have made it necessary for a few pictures to appear somewhat out of sequence.

1. VILLA AND GARDEN. 4 7/8 x 7 9/16.

1 *verso*. FRAGMENT OF PRISON SKETCH.

2. ARCHITECTURAL COMPLEX. 7 1/2 x 5 9/16.

3. CORNER OF COURT WITH FOUR FIGURES. 5 7/8 x 5 1/2.

4. ARCHITECTURAL COMPLEX WITH ORNAMENTAL TROPHY. 10 1/16 x 7 1/16.

6. ARCHITECTURAL COMPLEX OF GALLERIES AND ARCADES. 16 9/16 x 21 13/16.

5. Interior with arches and piers. 7 3/16 x 10.

5 *verso*. INTERIOR WITH CIRCULAR COLONNADE AND FOUNTAIN.

7. Design for title page. 15 1/2 x 20 7/16.

8. DESIGN FOR TITLE PAGE. 20 X 29 3/8.

9

7 *verso*.   STANDING NUDE MALE FIGURE. 15 1/2 x 20 7/16.

9. CAPRICCIO. 14 1/2 x 20 3/16.

11

10.   GONDOLA. 11 5/8 x 26 13/16.

13

10 *verso*.   Ornament with sun and star motifs; decorative frames. 11 5/8 x 26 13/16.

14

12. Design for wall panel. 12 13/16 x 14 3/4.

15

12 *verso*.　Sᴋᴇᴛᴄʜ ꜰᴏʀ ᴛᴀʙʟᴇ. 12 13/16 x 14 3/4.

11. DESIGN FOR WALL PANEL. 11 9/16 x 9 5/16.

13. WALL PANEL. 11 5/16 x 11 1/16.

14. DECORATIVE SHELL (?) FORM. 9 11/16 x 7 1/4.

15. PRISON INTERIOR. 8 7/16 x 5 15/16.

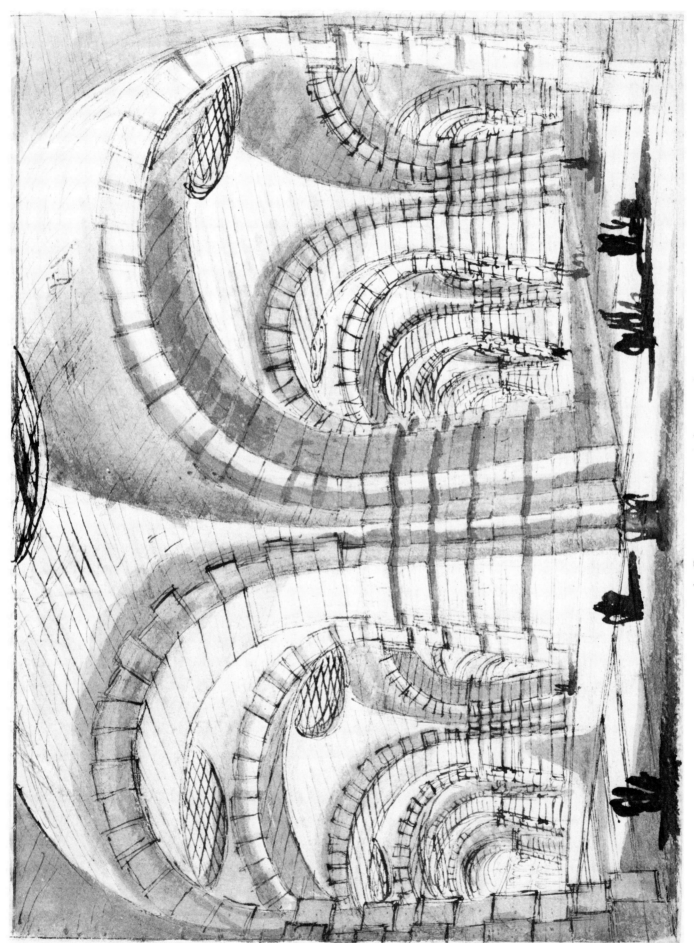

16. PRISON INTERIOR. 7 3/16 x 9 11/16.

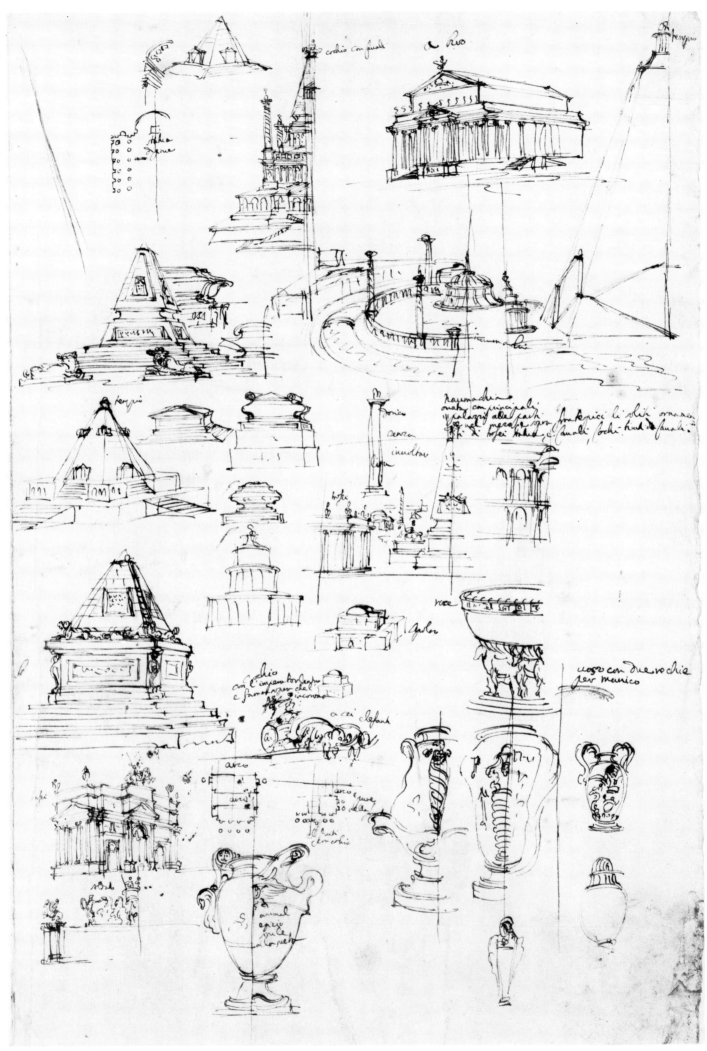

17. SHEET OF SKETCHES. 16 3/8 x 11 1/8.

18.   SHEET OF SKETCHES. 16 5/16 x 11 1/16.

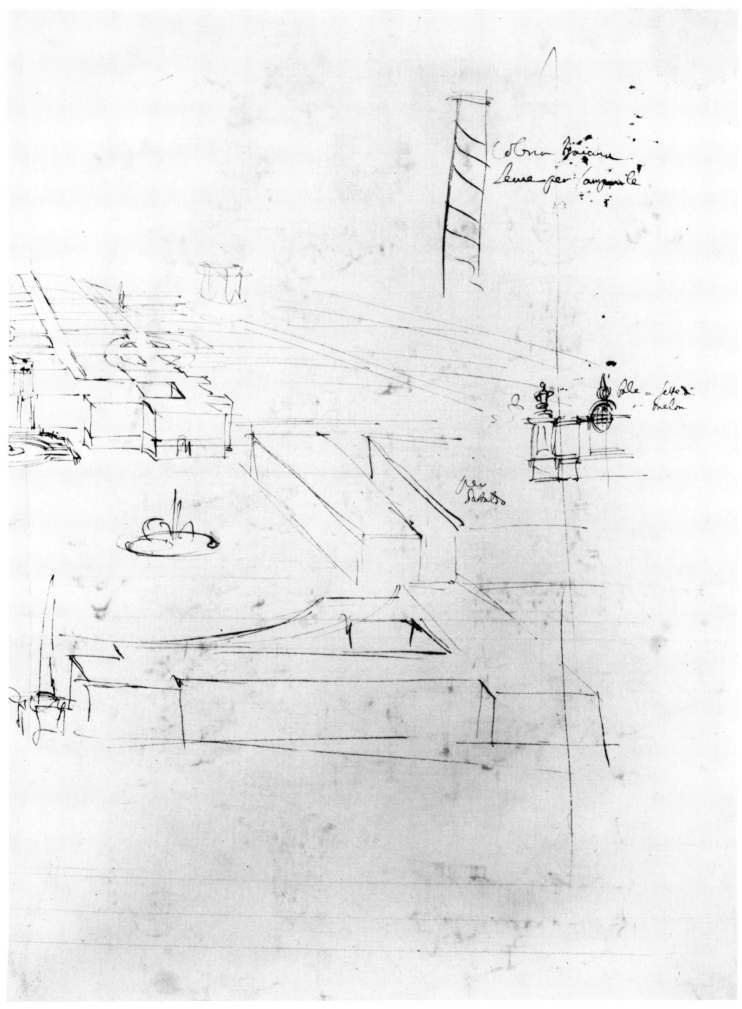

17 *verso.* LAYOUT OF FORMAL GARDEN.

18 *verso*. VILLA AND GARDEN.

19.   CAPITAL WITH CONFRONTED SPHINXES. 3 1/2 x 5 7/16.

20.   CAPITAL WITH CONFRONTED SPHINXES. 3 1/16 x 3 3/8.

21. DOLPHIN CAPITAL. 4 x 9.

21 *verso*.   ARCHITECTURAL FRAGMENT WITH SPHINX HEADS AND PUTTI.

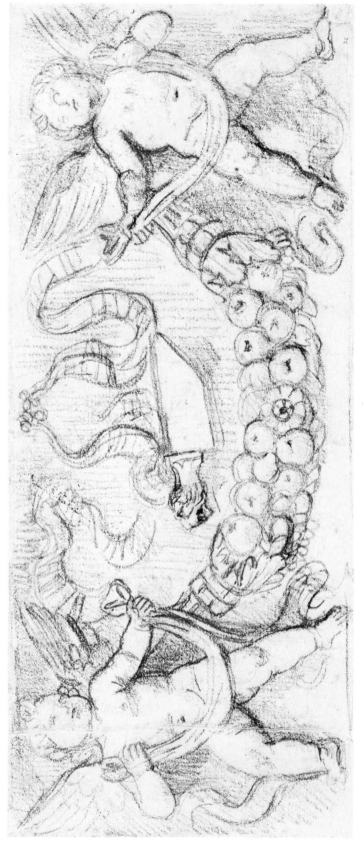

24. FRIEZE MOTIF. 4 3/4 x 11 3/16.

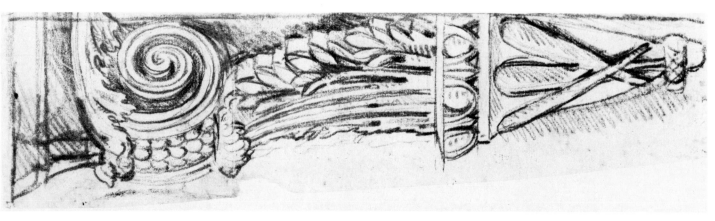

22. BRACKET. 9 5/16 x 2 1/2.

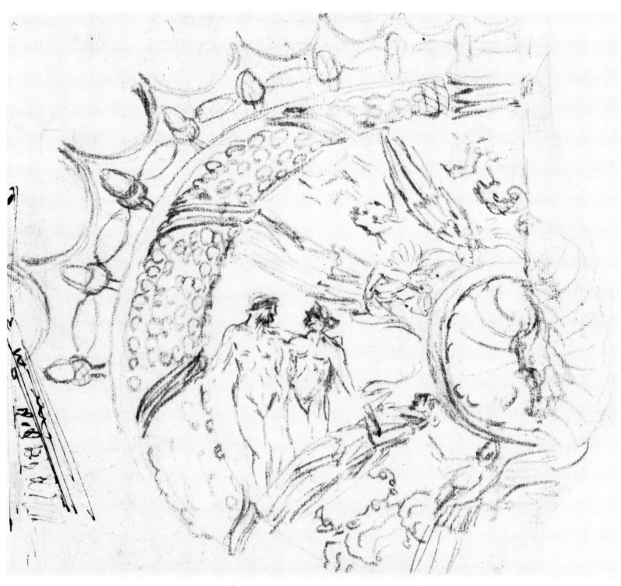

23. DECORATIVE SHIELD. 5 3/4 x 5 11/16.

25. EGG-AND-DART MOLDING. 4 13/16 x 13 3/8.

26. ACANTHUS LEAF. 7 5/16 x 11 15/16.

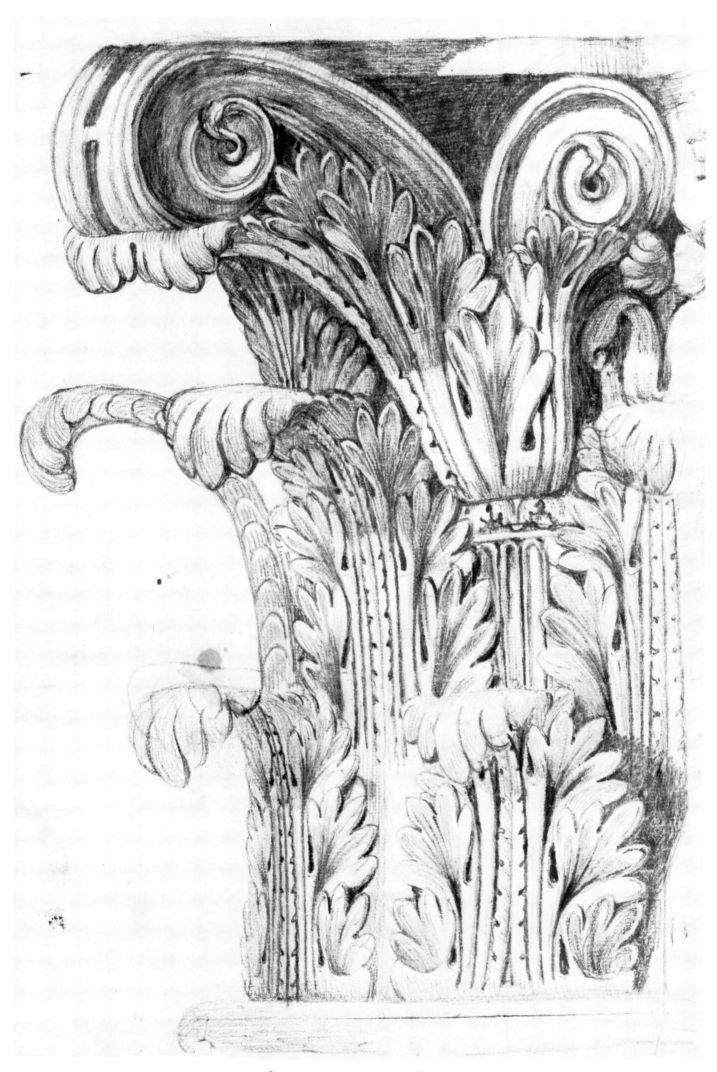

27.   CORINTHIAN CAPITAL. 15 7/16 x 10 1/2.

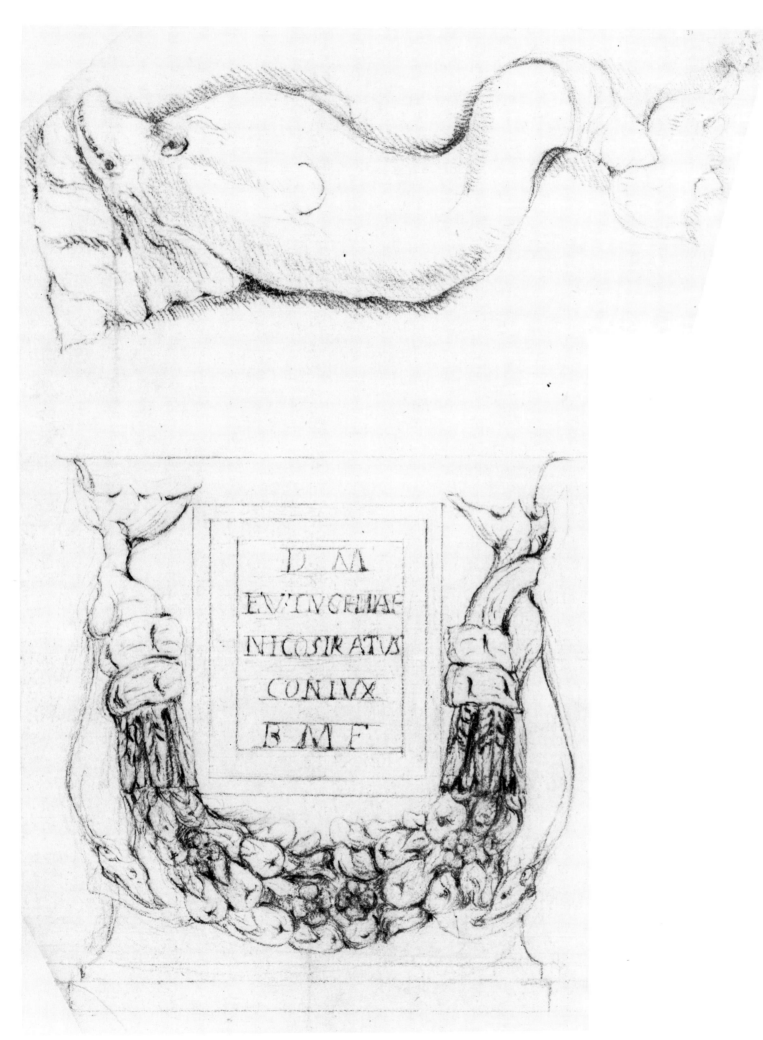

28. Funerary monument. 10 7/8 x 8 3/8.

29.   CLASSICAL HEAD; TWO HEADS OF RAMS. 5 3/8 x 6 13/16.

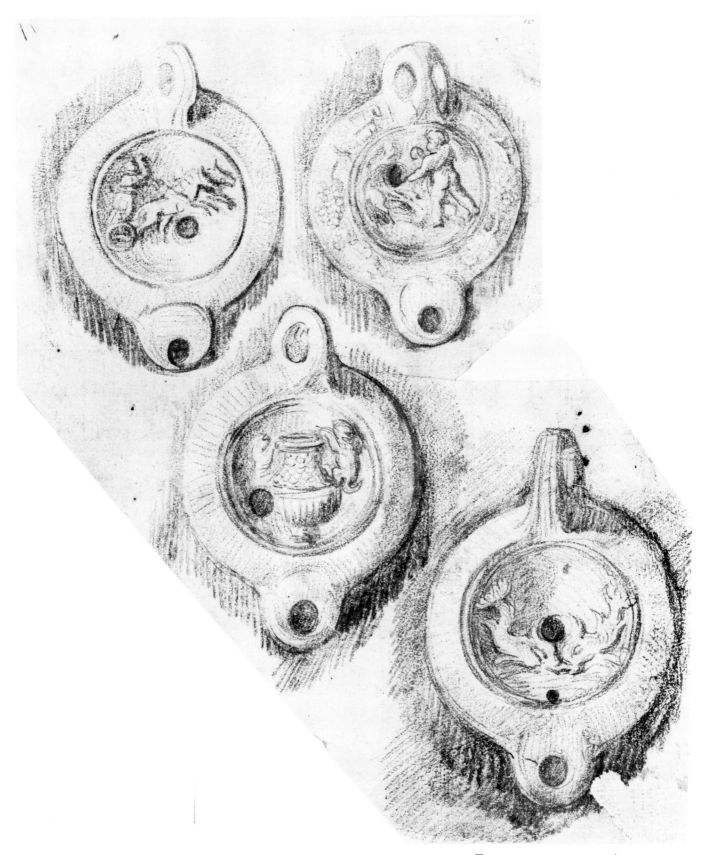

30. FOUR ANTIQUE LAMPS. 9 3/4 x 7.

31.   HEAD OF BEARDED MAN THREE-QUARTERS LEFT. 6 1/2 x 4 5/16.

32.   HEAD OF BEARDED MAN THREE-QUARTERS RIGHT. 6 1/2 x 4 3/8.

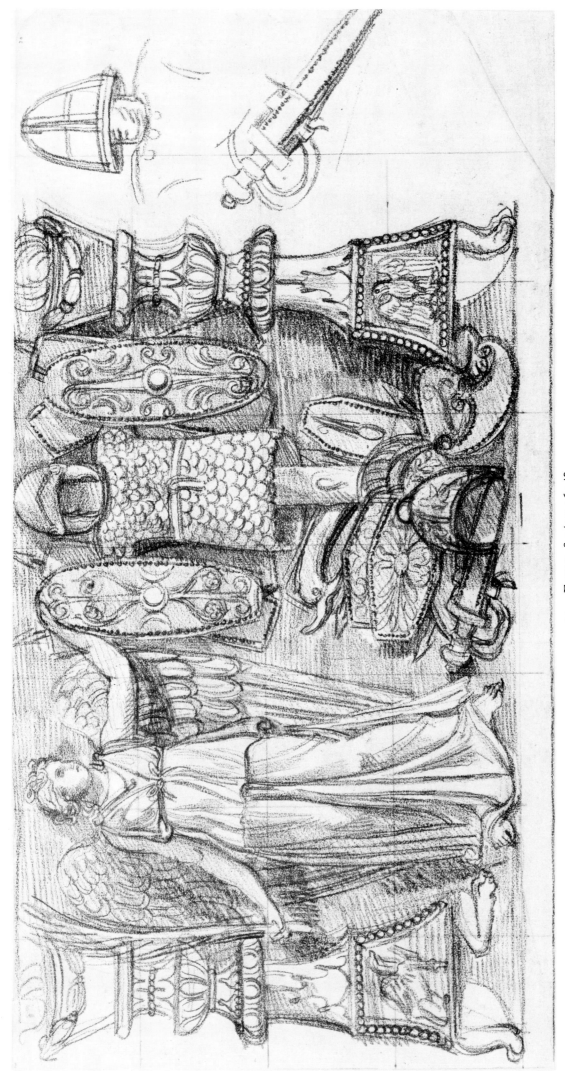

33. Frieze. 8 1/2 x 16 1/8.

35. LUNETTE WITH TROPHIES; WINGED SERPENTS AND DOLPHINS IN SPANDRELS. 10 7/16 x 22.

34.   STUDIES FROM THE ANTIQUE. 18 5/16 x 13 3/4.

36.   FRIEZE MOTIF. 2 15/16 X 9 1/4.

37.   SKETCH AFTER ANTIQUE RELIEF WITH FOUR HEADS, TORCHES, AND STARS. 7 X 5 3/4.

42. SKETCH OF CAPITAL WITH DOLPHIN AND ACANTHUS. 5 x 9 9/16.

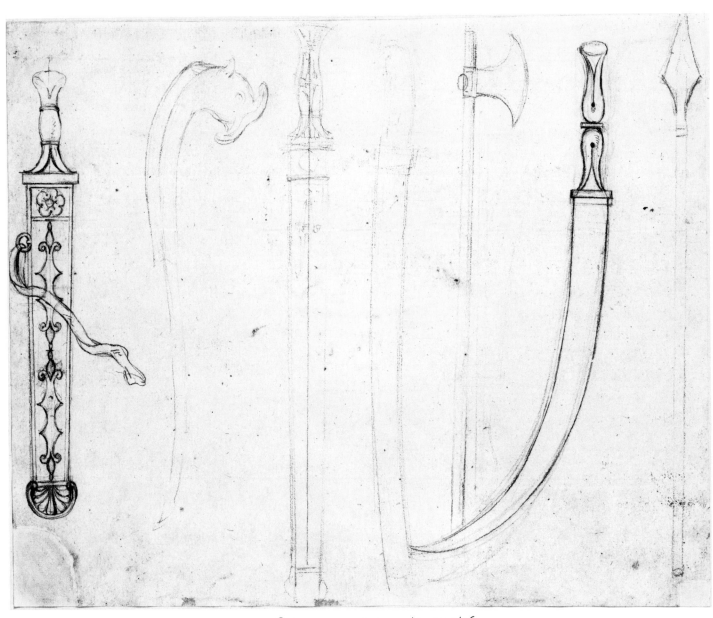

41. CLASSICAL WEAPONS. 10 3/4 x 13 5/16.

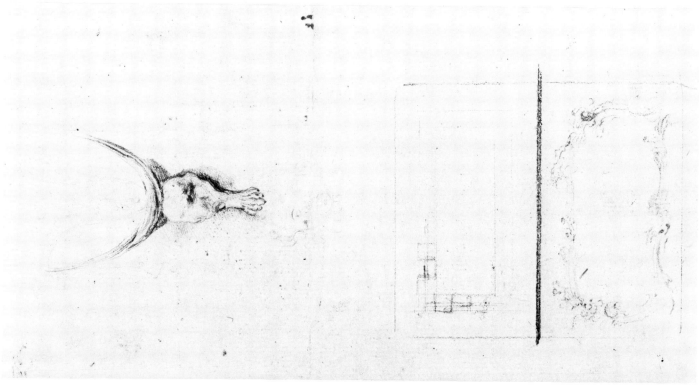

42 *verso.*   ANIMAL CLAW AND LEG; PUTTO HEAD; ROCOCO PANEL.

38.   PEDIMENTED NICHE WITH FRIEZE BELOW. 8 11/16 x 5 1/4.

43. SIX MASKS. 8 x 13 7/16.

39. LION-CLAW PEDESTAL AND SHALLOW URN. 6 13/16 x 8 1/2.

45.　Mask. 4 1/4 x 3 1/8.

44.　Three masks. 7 7/8 x 10 1/8.

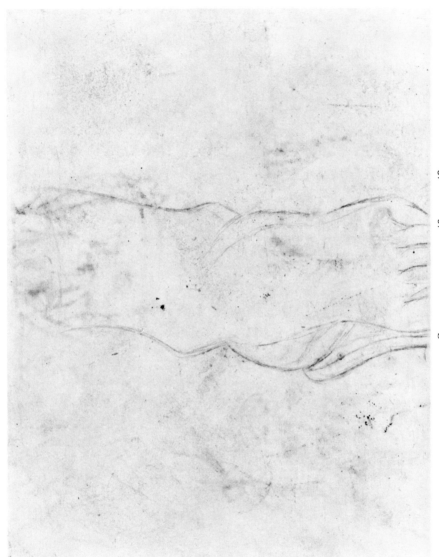

46. COLUMN. 10 5/8 x 2 11/16.

44 verso. SANDALED FOOT. 7 7/8 x 10 1/8.

40. HORNED GROTESQUE WITH PROTRUDING
TONGUE. 2 5/16 x 2 13/16.

47.   SKETCHES OF MOLDINGS. 7 7/8 x 11 7/8.

47 *verso*.   PEDESTAL WITH SPHINX BASE OVER OUTLINE SKETCH OF LION.

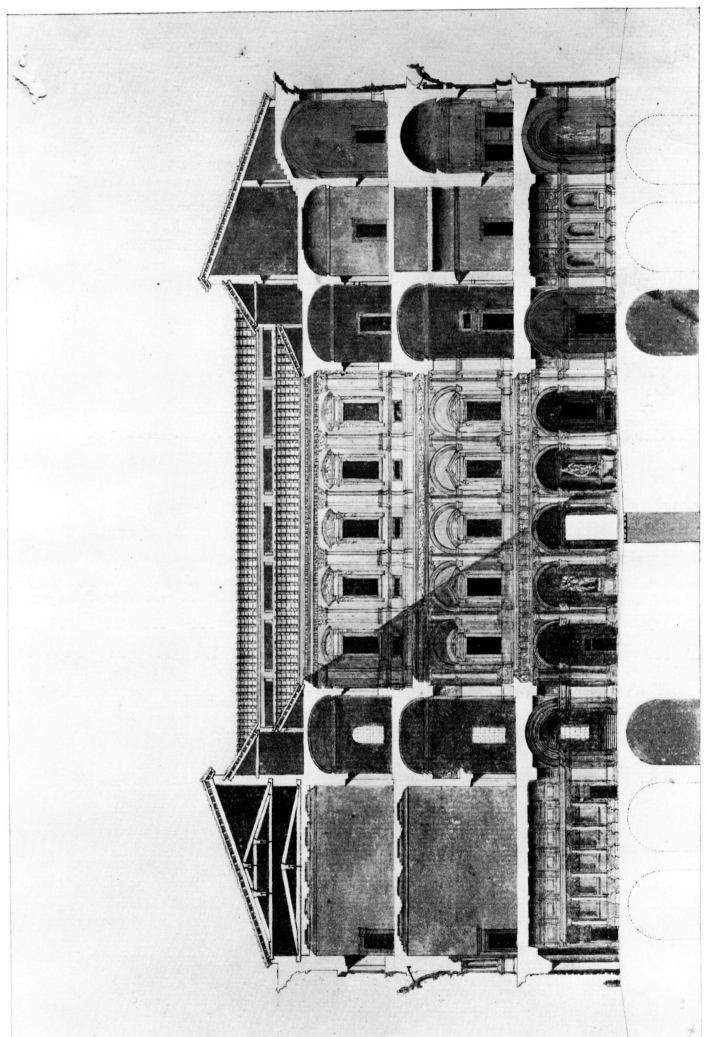

48. FARNESE PALACE. LONGITUDINAL SECTION. 8 3/4 × 12 11/16.

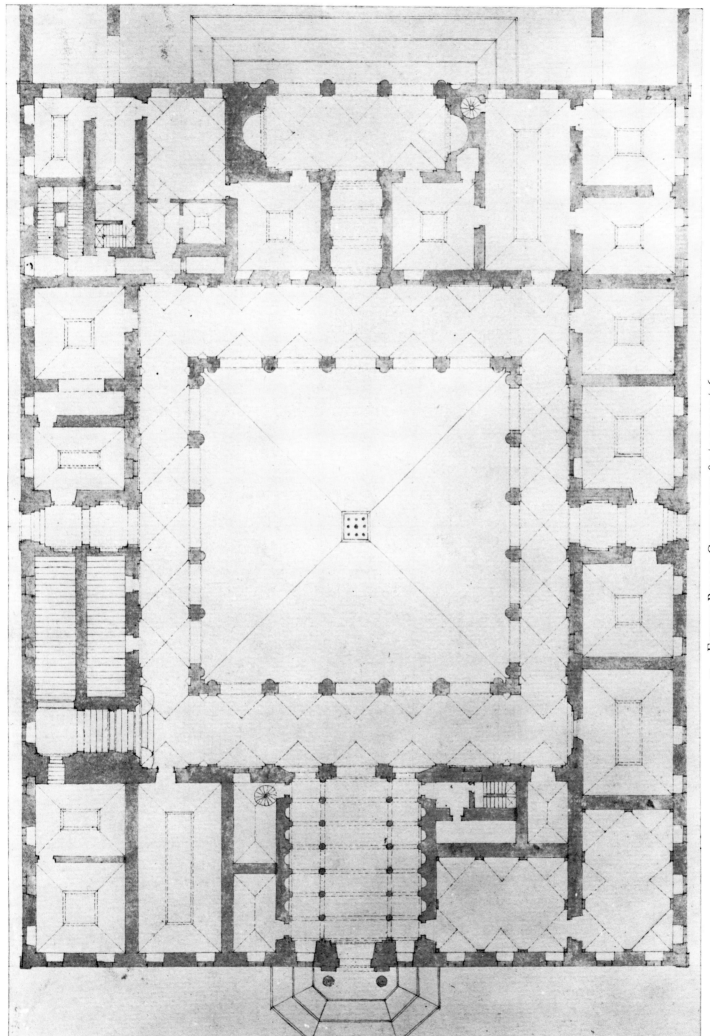

49. Farnese Palace. Ground plan. 8 3/4 x 12 13/16.

47

50. Santa Maria Aventina. Panel with emblems of the Order of Malta. 20 7/8 x 12 1/2.

51.   SANTA MARIA AVENTINA. DESIGN FOR LOWER PART OF HIGH ALTAR. 18 9/16 x 14 3/8.

52. SANTA MARIA AVENTINA. ORNAMENTS SHOWING SCABBARD
AND REZZONICO INSIGNIA. 6 1/4 x 2 13/16.

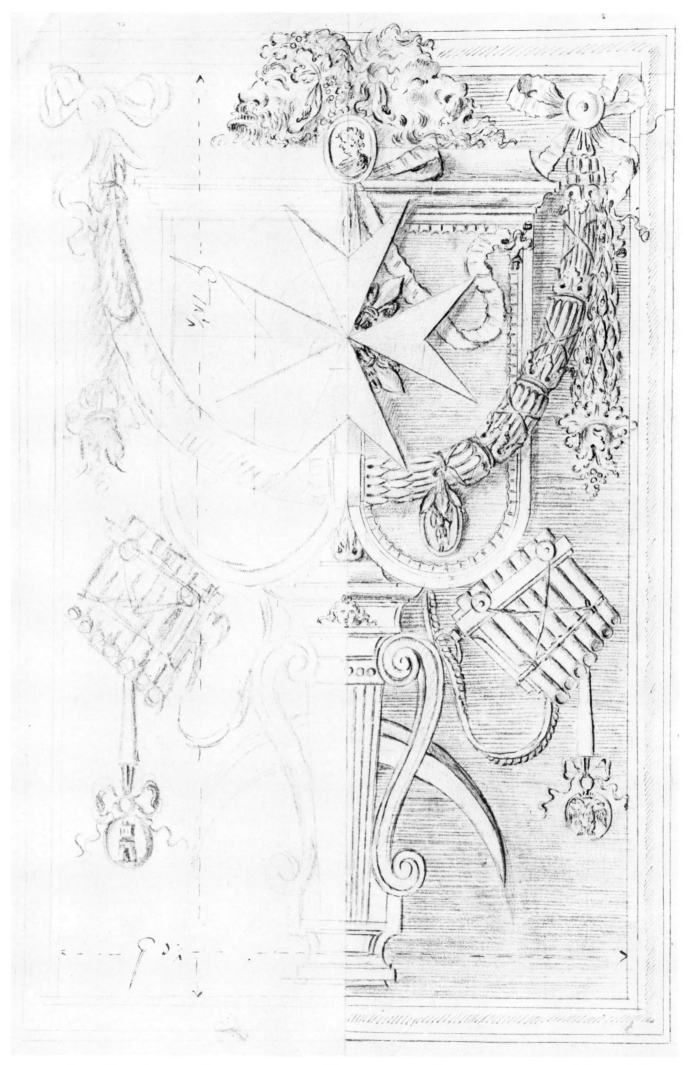

53.   SANTA MARIA AVENTINA. VERTICAL PANEL WITH MALTESE CROSS AND REZZONICO INSIGNIA. 15 13/16 X 10 7/16.

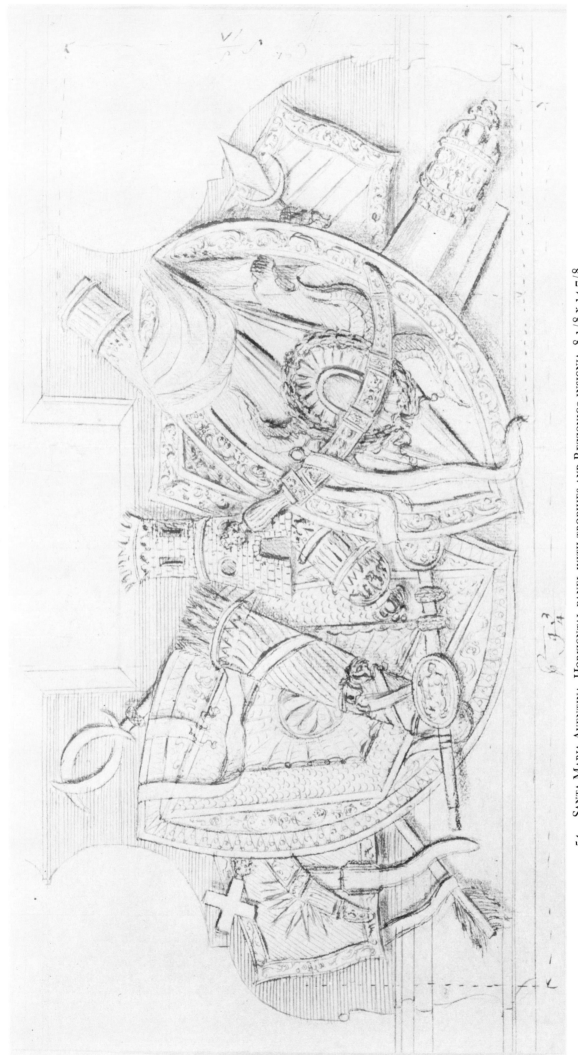

54. Santa Maria Aventina. Horizontal panel with trophies and Rezzonico insignia. 8 1/8 x 14 7/8.

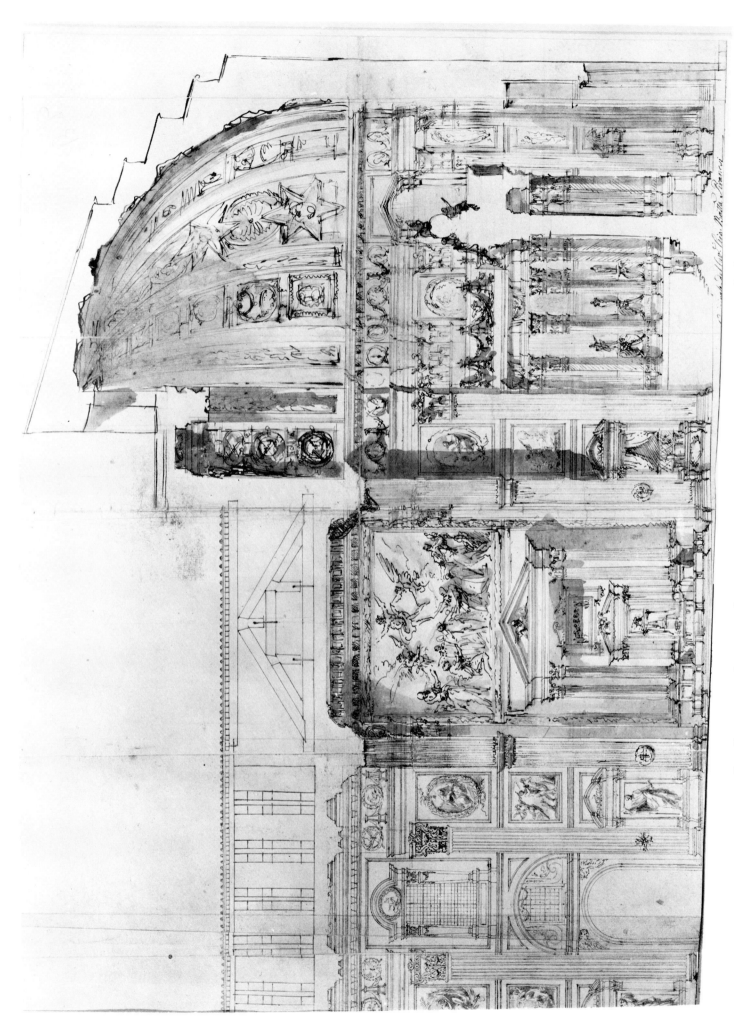

55. SAN GIOVANNI IN LATERANO. LONGITUDINAL SECTION THROUGH LENGTH OF NAVE. 21 x 58 1/4.
The detail above shows the right end of the sheet, containing the areas certainly drawn by Piranesi himself. The entire sheet, moving from left to right, is reproduced in four sections on the following four pages.

53

San Giovanni Laterano

FIRST SECTION (EXTREME LEFT) OF NO. 55.

SECOND SECTION OF NO. 55.

THIRD SECTION OF NO. 55.

FOURTH SECTION OF NO. 55.

56. SAN GIOVANNI IN LATERANO. LONGITUDINAL SECTION BEGINNING AT TRANSEPT. 12 9/16 X 21 3/8.

57. San Giovanni in Laterano. Section through choir. 13 5/8 x 15 1/4.

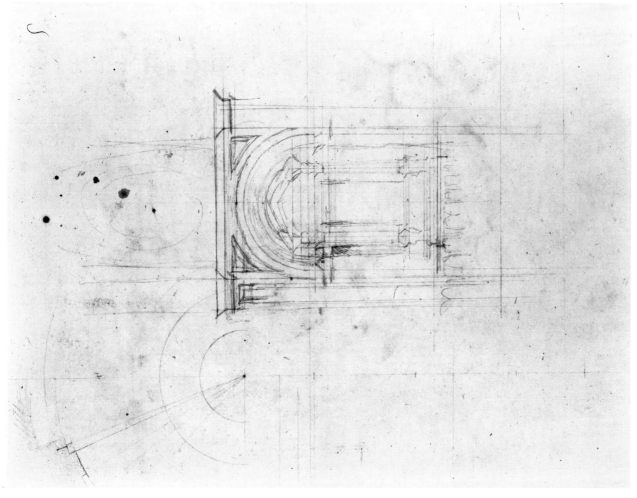

58 *verso.* San Giovanni in Laterano. Sketch for niche of choir wall.

58. San Giovanni in Laterano. Sketch for choir wall; putti. 13 11/16 x 10 1/4.

59.   DESIGN FOR MANTELPIECE. 6 1/16 x 11 3/4.

61.   DESIGN FOR MANTELPIECE WITH CONFRONTED ELEPHANT HEADS; PILASTER. 8 3/8 x 12 11/16.

Candélabre à deux cygnes

façade à tête

60. SKETCHES FOR MANTELPIECE AND TABLE. 11 1/16 x 13 3/16.

62. DESIGN FOR MANTELPIECE WITH CORNER MEDALLION; SEATED FIGURE. 6 3/8 x 9 5/8.

63. DESIGN FOR MANTELPIECE. 9 1/8 x 14 5/16.

64. DESIGN FOR MANTELPIECE. 8 x 11 3/8.

65. DESIGN FOR MANTELPIECE. 7 15/16 x 14 3/16.

66. DESIGN FOR MANTELPIECE. 7 15/16 x 12 1/4.

67. DESIGN FOR MANTELPIECE. 6 15/16 x 12 3/16.

66 verso. Corner of temple and adjacent building with tile roof.

68.　DESIGN FOR MANTELPIECE WITH EGYPTIAN ORNAMENT. 8 9/16 x 12 3/16.

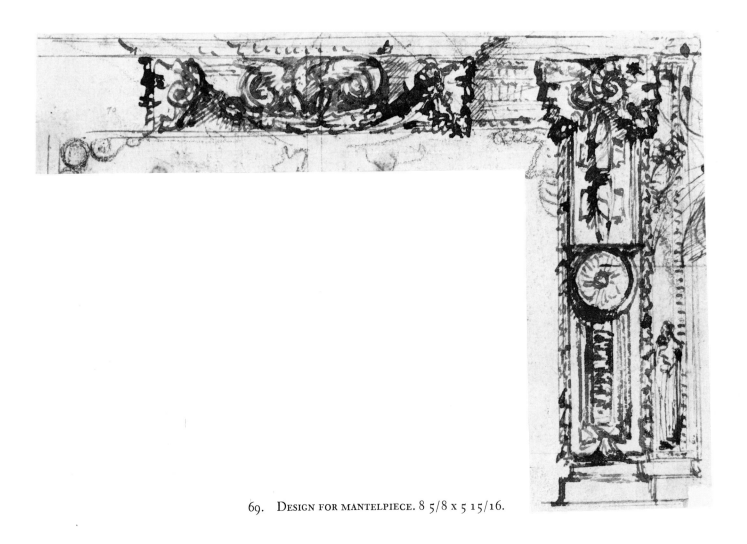

69.　DESIGN FOR MANTELPIECE. 8 5/8 x 5 15/16.

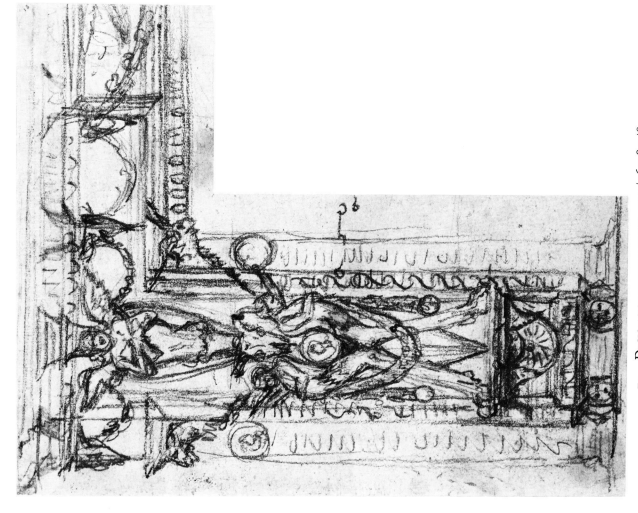

72. Design for mantelpiece. 10 9/16 x 8 1/8.

70. Design for mantelpiece. 7 11/16 x 6 11/16.

71. Designs for ornamental frame and for cartouche. 7 1/8 x 10 3/8.

71 *verso.*   FRAGMENT OF DESIGN FOR TITLE PAGE.

73. DESIGN FOR MANTELPIECE. 3 7/16 x 4 13/16.

74. DESIGN FOR MANTELPIECE. 3 15/16 x 6.

76. DESIGN FOR MANTELPIECE. 3 7/8 x 2 9/16.

75. THREE SKETCHES FOR MANTELPIECE. 7 1/4 x 12 3/4.

77.   DESIGN FOR MANTELPIECE. 9 5/16 x 16 5/16.

78. DESIGN FOR MANTELPIECE. 6 1/4 x 5 7/8.

79. DESIGN FOR MANTELPIECE. 5 15/16 x 6 3/4.

80 *verso.* DESIGN FOR MANTELPIECE.

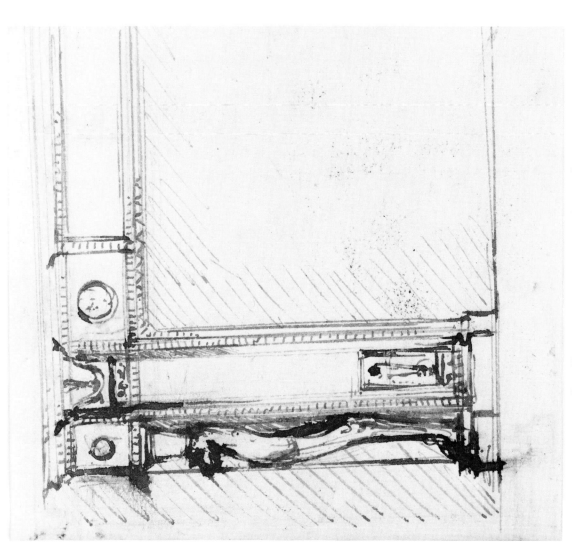

80. DESIGN FOR MANTELPIECE. 6 1/2 x 6.

82. Design for Mantelpiece. 4 13/16 x 5.

81. Design for Mantelpiece. 5 7/8 x 7 1/8.

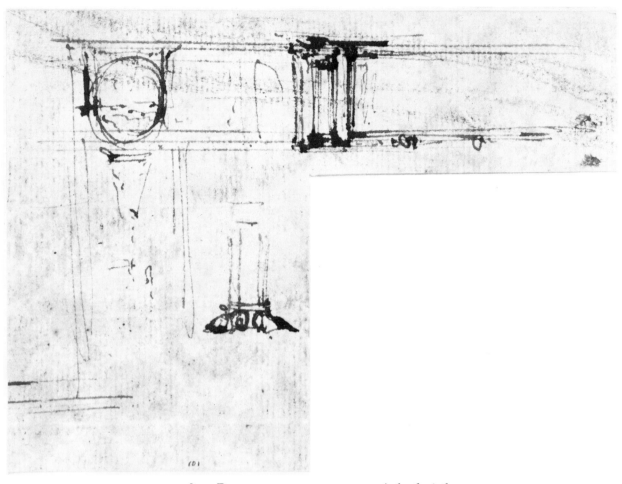

83. DESIGN FOR MANTELPIECE. 4 11/16 x 6 9/16.

84. DESIGN FOR MANTELPIECE. 7 13/16 x 16 9/16.

85. Design for mantelpiece. 9 11/16 x 13 3/8.

86. Design for mantelpiece and chair. 7 1/8 x 13 15/16.

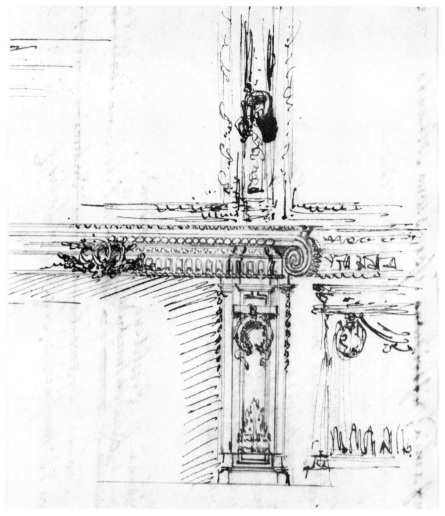

88. DESIGN FOR MANTELPIECE. 5 13/16 x 5 1/16.

87. SKETCH FOR MANTELPIECE. 5 3/4 x 7 1/2.

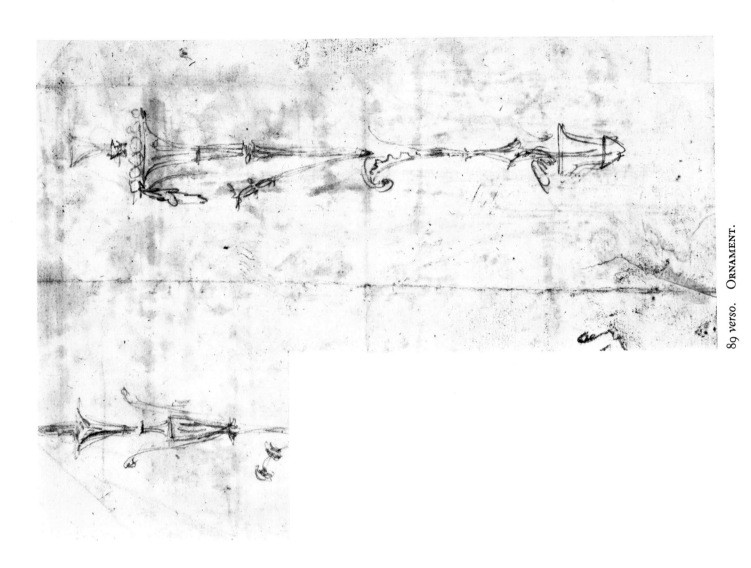

89 *verso.* ORNAMENT.

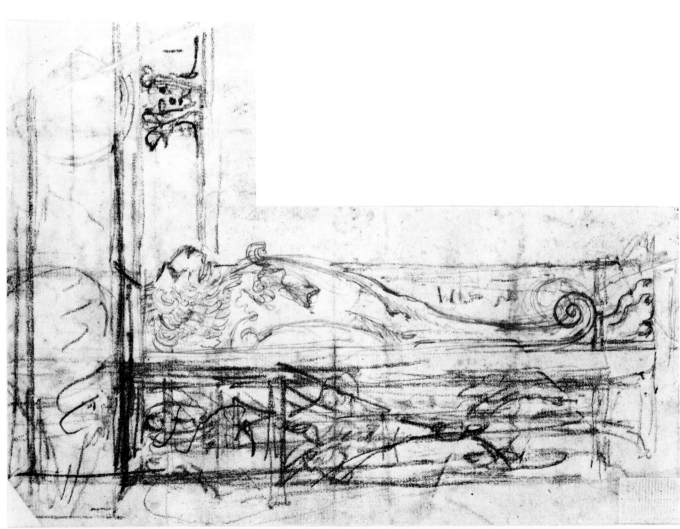

89. SKETCH FOR MANTELPIECE. 10 x 7 3/16.

90.   SKETCH FOR MANTELPIECE. 4 x 3 9/16.

91.   SKETCH FOR MANTELPIECE. 2 3/4 x 4 11/16.

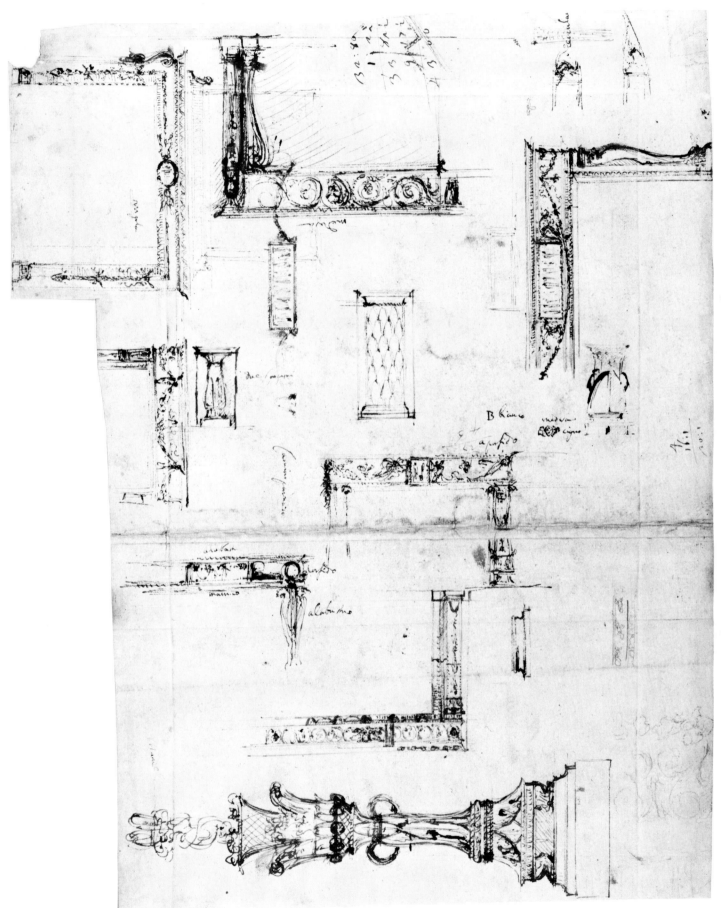

92. SKETCHES FOR MANTELPIECES AND CANDELABRA. 17 1/4 x 25 1/8.

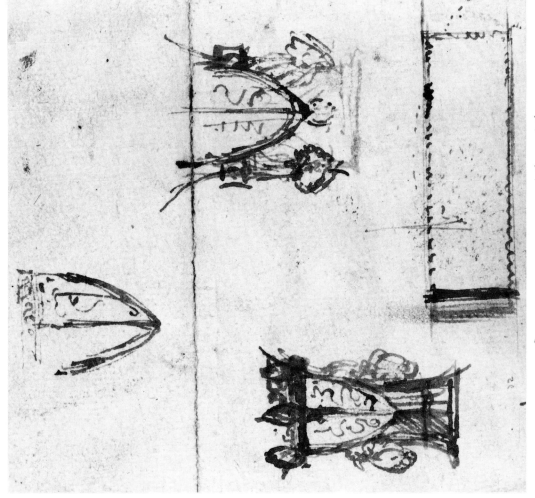

94. Sketches for ornament. 5 9/16 x 5 1/16.

93. Two sketches for candelabra. 8 3/8 x 1 11/16.

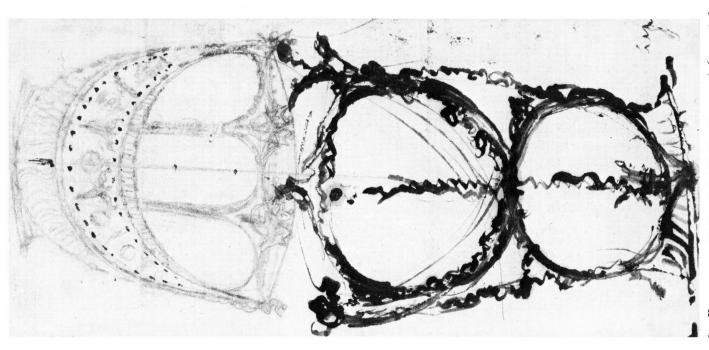

96. DESIGNS FOR SEDAN CHAIR AND COACH. 11 11/16 x 5 3/16.

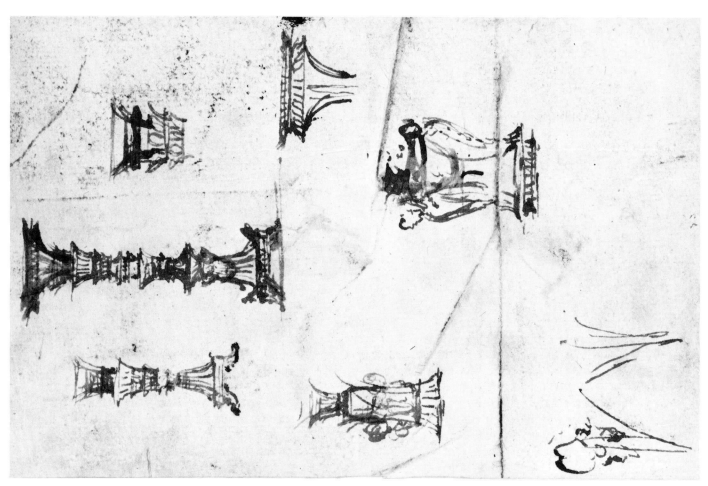

95. SKETCHES FOR CANDELABRA. 8 3/16 x 5 3/16.

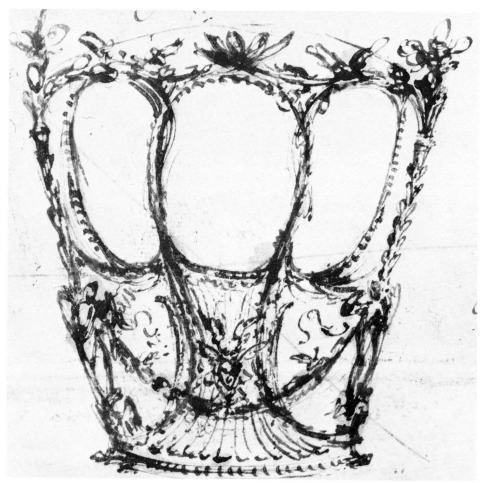

97. DESIGN FOR COACH. 5 1/8 x 5 7/16.

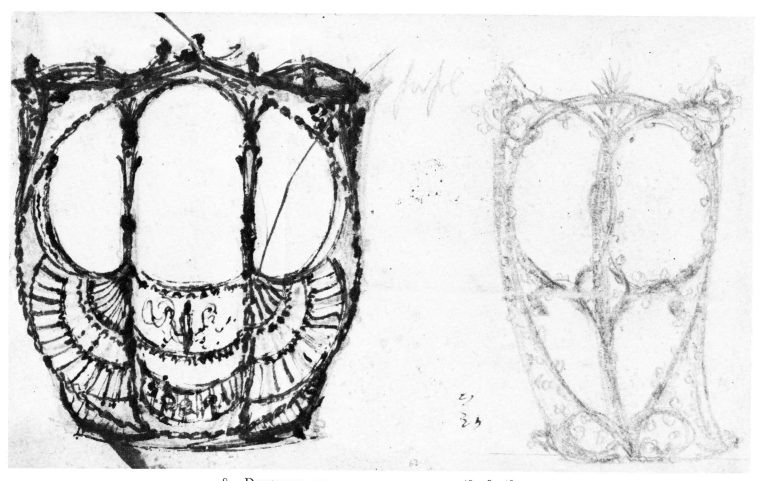

98. DESIGNS FOR COACH AND SEDAN CHAIR. 4 7/8 x 8 3/8.

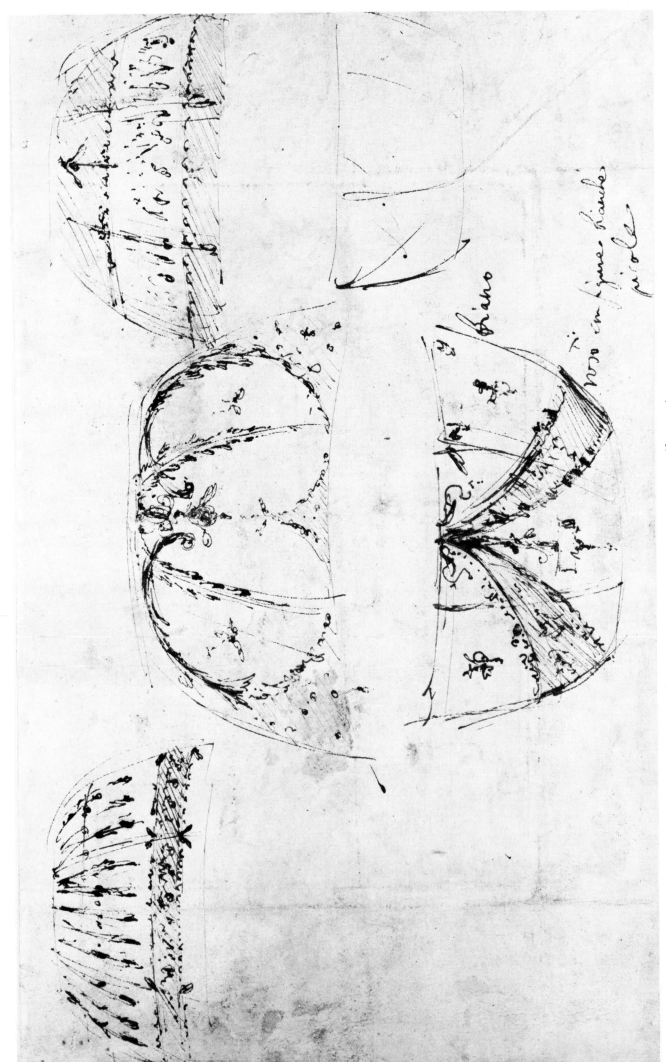

99. Sketches for decoration of coaches. 9 1/8 x 14 3/4.

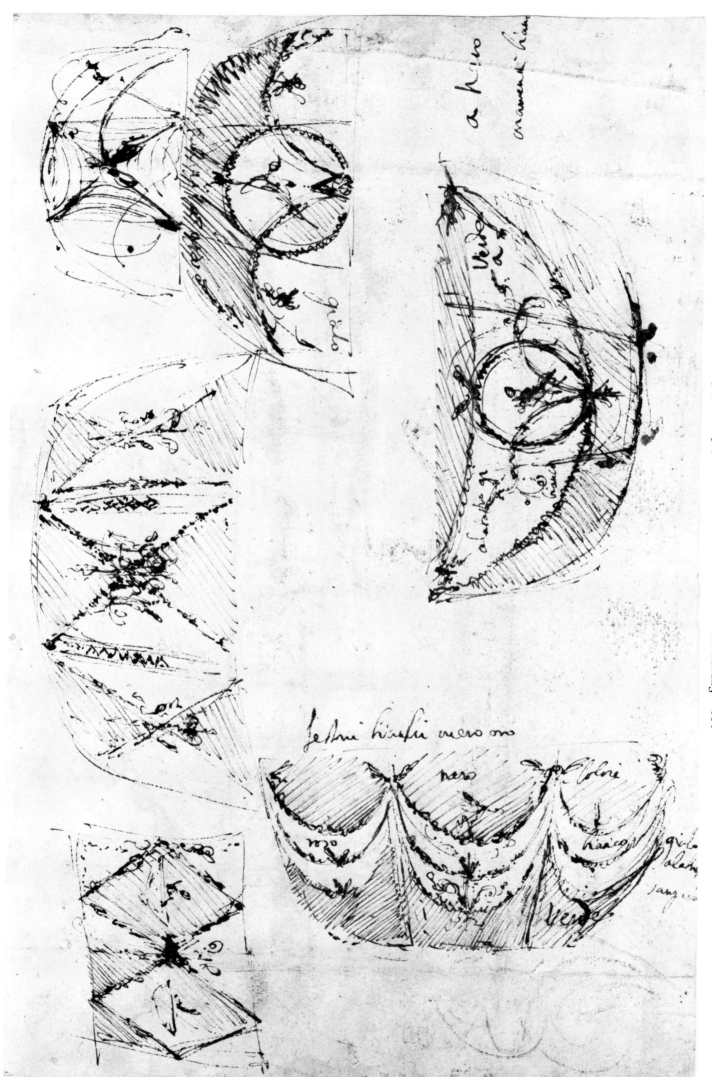

101. SKETCH FOR ORNAMENT WITH GRIFFIN
ON BASE. 3 11/16 x 2 5/16.

102. CHAIR WITH SHIELD BACK.
3 1/16 x 1 13/16.

105. ORNAMENT WITH INTERTWINED
DOLPHINS. 2 1/8 x 2 3/16.

103.   DESIGN FOR CLOCK. 4 1/2 x 2 7/16.

104.   DESIGN FOR STOOL. 2 13/16 x 4 5/16.

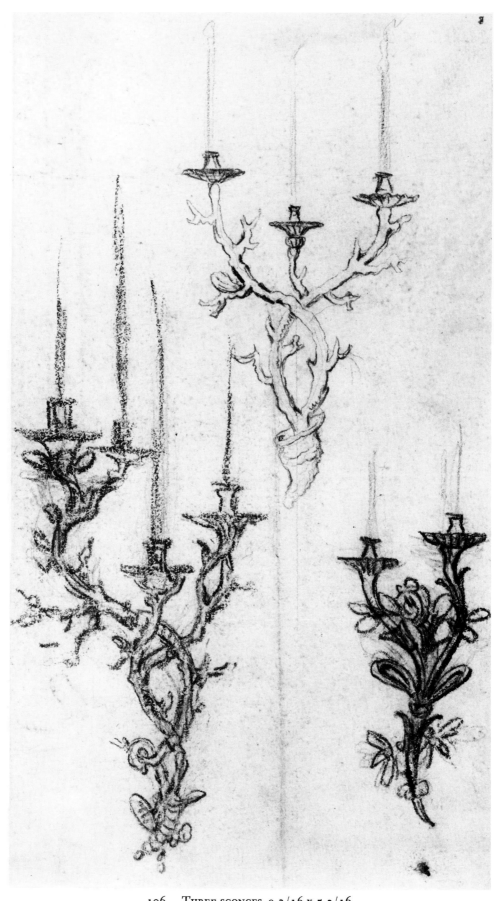

106.   THREE SCONCES. 9 3/16 x 5 3/16.

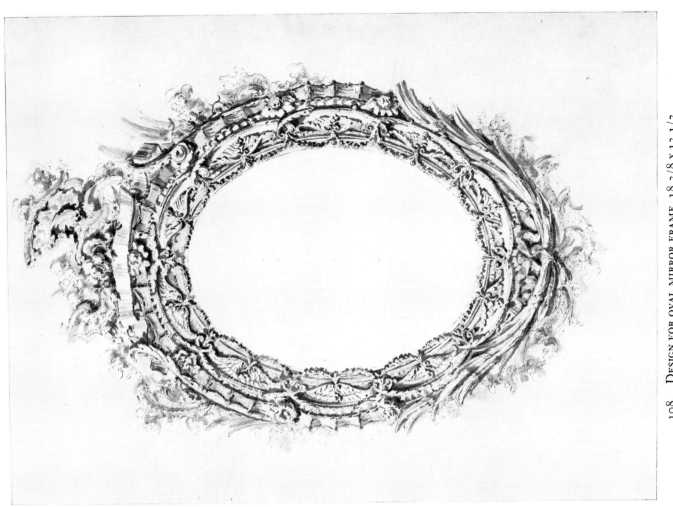

108. Design for oval mirror frame. 18 3/8 x 13 1/2.

107. Design for oval mirror frame. 18 9/16 x 13 1/2.

93

109. Design for rectangular frame for oval mirror. 19 11/16 x 15 3/16.

112.   FOUNTAIN. 9 3/4 x 5 5/16.

110. DESIGN FOR WALL MONUMENT WITH PAPAL AND DUCAL CROWNS. 13 3/16 x 7 3/16.

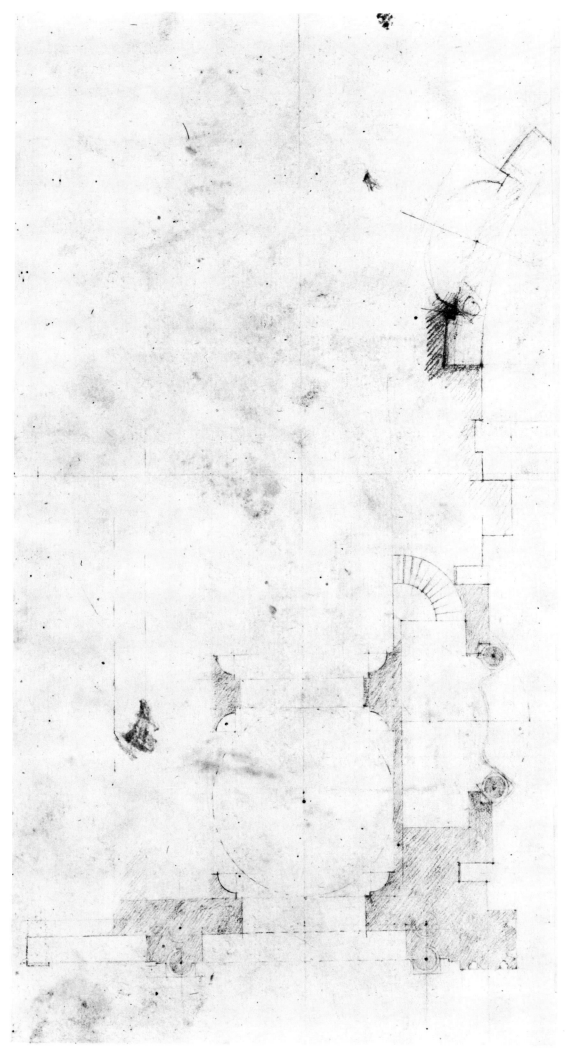

110 *verso*.   FRAGMENT OF GROUND PLAN.

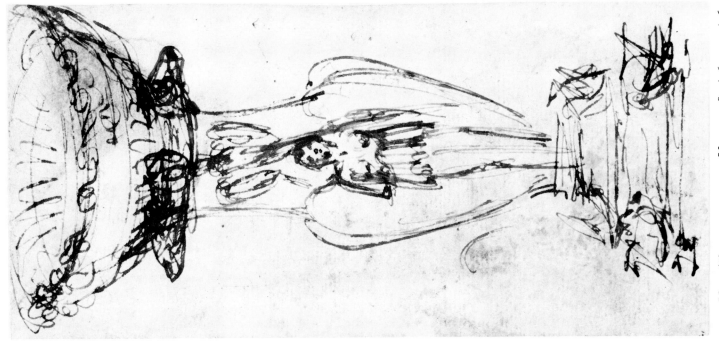

113. Vase (?) with figure of Victory. 8 9/16 x 3 15/16.

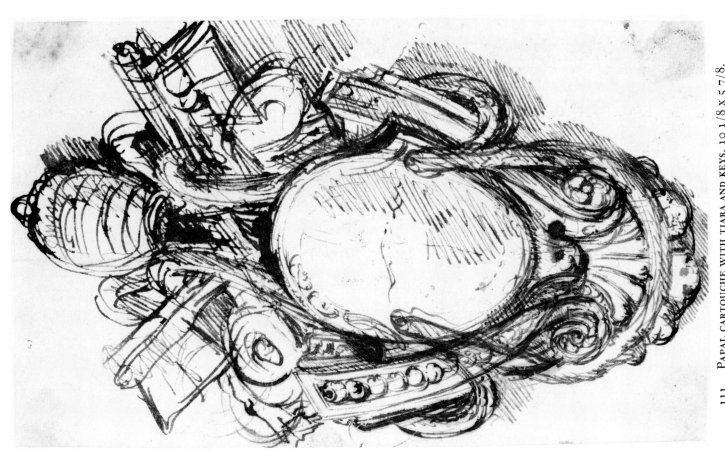

111. Papal cartouche with tiara and keys. 10 1/8 x 5 7/8.

114. TABERNACLE. 5 5/16 x 3 3/4.

116. SKETCH OF FIGURE AND VASES. 6 x 10.

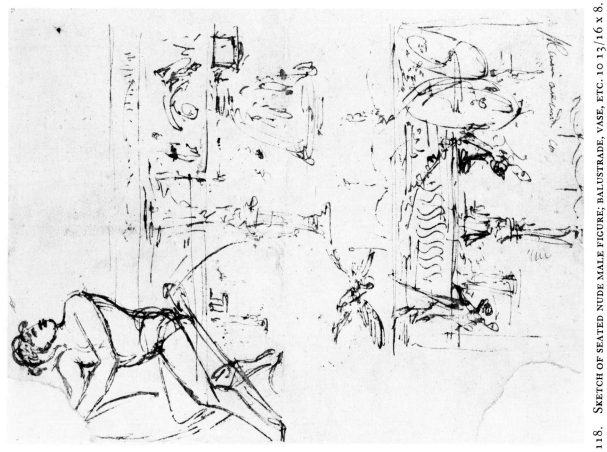

118. SKETCH OF SEATED NUDE MALE FIGURE; BALUSTRADE, VASE, ETC. 10 13/16 x 8.

115. PERSPECTIVE SKETCH FOR DECORATIVE PANEL. 9 7/8 x 8 7/8.

119. Sketch of balustrade, column, garland. 5 x 10 1/4.

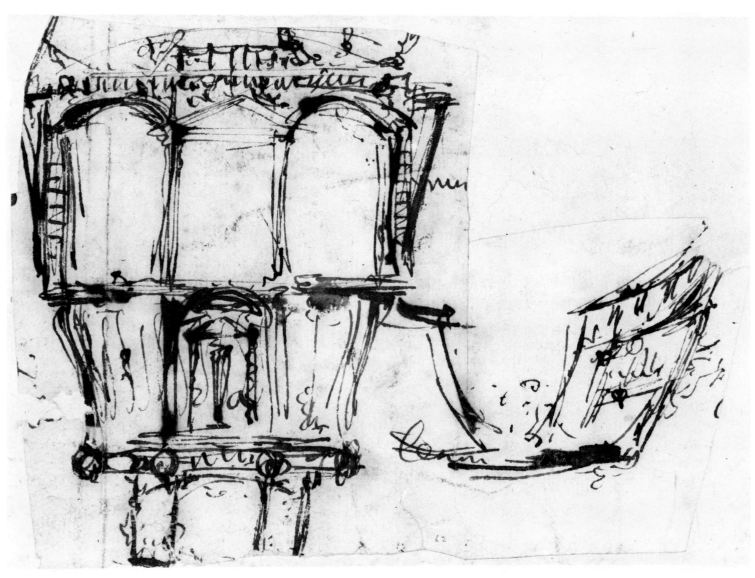

120. Sketch for prow of ship (?). 5 7/8 x 8 1/8.

117.   SKETCH OF HEAD AND SHOULDERS OF MAN. 3 3/16 x 3 1/8.

121.   CARTOUCHE. 2 3/4 x 5 3/16.

122. Sketches of head and shoulders of bearded man. 6 3/8 x 5 1/2.

123. SKETCHES OF ORNAMENT. 8 5/16 x 11.

124. VASE. 8 5/16 x 4 13/16.

125. VASE. 7 11/16 x 6 3/8.

126. DESIGN FOR BOOKPLATE FOR CARDINAL
OF ALBANI FAMILY. 4 11/16 X 3 3/4.

127. DESIGN FOR BOOKPLATE FOR CARDINAL
OF ALBANI FAMILY. 4 13/16 X 4 1/4.

127 *verso.* FRAGMENT OF DESIGN FOR CARDINAL'S ARMS.

131. SKETCH OF HADRIANIC MEDALLION FROM THE ARCH OF
CONSTANTINE. 4 1/4 X 5 3/16.

128.   STUDY OF STATUE OF DRAPED SEATED FEMALE FIGURE. 9 5/16 x 6 1/4.

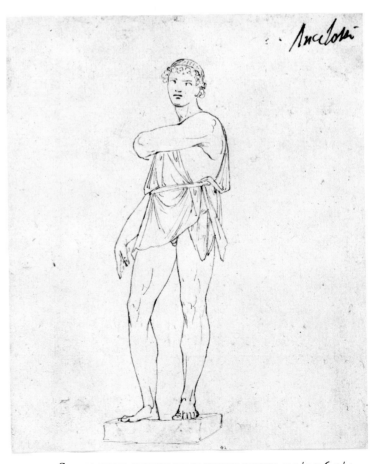

129.   STUDY AFTER STATUE OF DRAPED STANDING FEMALE
FIGURE. 8 3/4 x 6 1/16.

130.   STUDY AFTER STATUE OF STANDING YOUTH. 7 1/2 x 6 1/4.

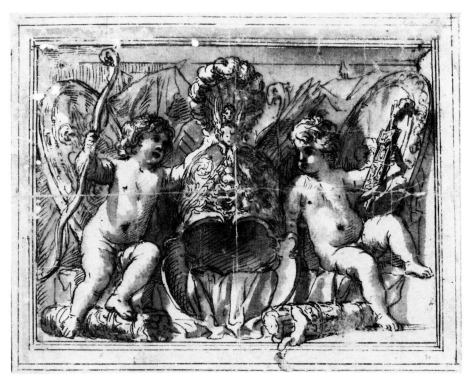

133. PUTTI WITH HELMET AND TROPHIES. 5 11/16 x 7 7/16.

132. MEDLEY OF CLASSICAL FRAGMENTS. 15 5/16 x 18 15/16.

A-1. ARCHITECTURAL FANTASY. 10 9/16 x 16 7/8.

A-2. CENTRAL VIEW OF A CHURCH INTERIOR. 7 3/8 x 9 11/16.

A-3. ASSASSINATION SCENE. 9 9/16 x 7 5/16.

A-5.　Santa Maria Aventina. Sketch for the high altar. 4 5/8 x 4 9/16.

A-4. Architectural Fantasy. 9 5/16 x 12 15/16.

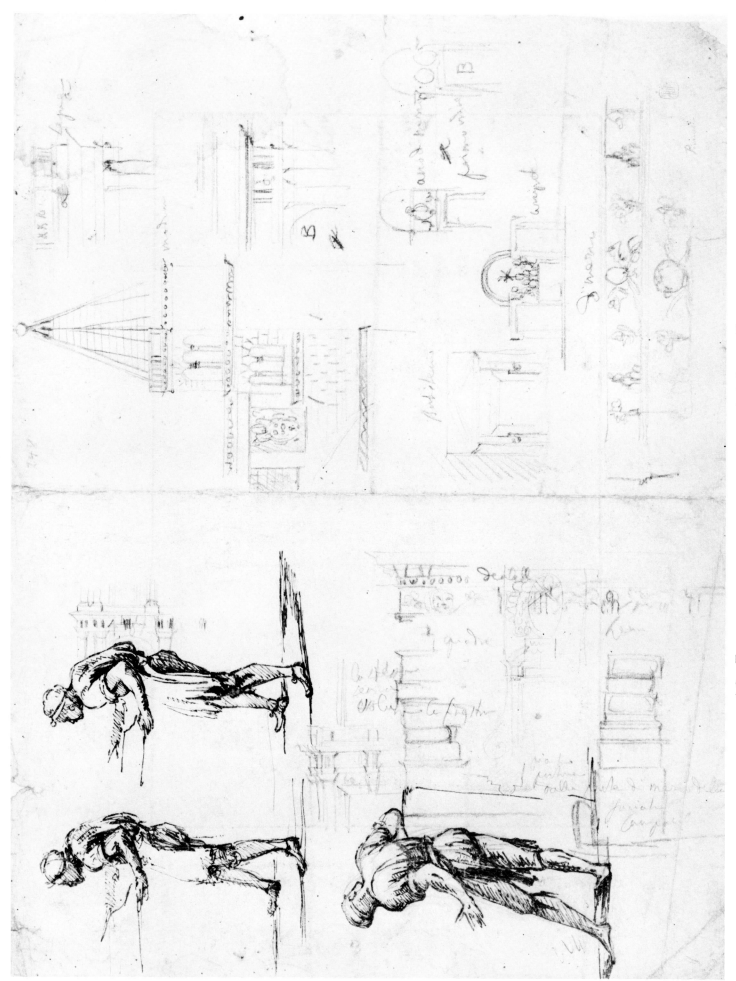

A-8. Three figures and architectural details. 16 9/16 x 21 5/8.

A-6. RUINS AT POZZUOLI. 19 5/16 x 30.

A-7.   TEMPLE OF ISIS AT POMPEII. 20 1/2 x 30 3/4.

117

A-9.   Figure studies. 9 1/16 x 5 1/2.

A-10.   Standing man gesturing with his right arm.
5 3/16 x 3 1/4.

A-12.   Domed church, obelisk at left. 4 3/8 x 7.
Collection of Mr. and Mrs. Eugene V. Thaw, Promised Gift to the Morgan Library

A-11. TEMPLE OF ISIS AT POMPEII. 20 1/8 x 30.
Collection of Mr. and Mrs. Eugene V. Thaw, Promised Gift to the Morgan Library

(on back) Veduta in angolo del tempio d' Giube